4th Workshop on Natural Language Processing Techniques for Educational Applications (NLPTEA 2017)

Taipei, Taiwan
1 December 2017

ISBN: 978-1-5108-5288-4

NLPTEA 2017

**The 4th Workshop on Natural Language Processing
Techniques for Educational Applications**

Proceedings of the NLPTEA 2017 Workshop

December 1, 2017
Taipei, Taiwan

Preface

Welcome to the 4th Workshop on Natural Language Processing Techniques for Educational Applications (NLPTEA 2017), with a Shared Task on Chinese Spelling Check.

The development of Natural Language Processing (NLP) has advanced to a level that affects the research landscape of many academic domains and has practical applications in many industrial sectors. On the other hand, educational environment has also been improved to impact the world society, such as the emergence of MOOCs (Massive Open Online Courses). With these trends, this workshop focuses on the NLP techniques applied to the educational environment. Research issues in this direction have gained more and more attention, examples including the activities like the workshops on Innovative Use of NLP for Building Educational Applications since 2005 and educational data mining conferences since 2008.

This is the fourth workshop held in the Asian area, with the first one NLPTEA 2014 workshop being held in conjunction with the 22nd International Conference on Computer in Education (ICCE 2014) from Nov. 30 to Dec. 4, 2014 in Japan. The second edition NLPTEA 2015 workshop was held in conjunction with the 53rd Annual Meeting of the Association for Computational Linguistics and the 7th International Joint Conference on Natural Language Processing (ACL-IJCNLP 2015) from July 26- 31 in Beijing, China. The third version NLPTEA 2016 workshop was held in conjunction with the 26th International Conference on Computational Linguistics (COLING 2016) from December 11- 16 in Osaka, Japan. This year, we continue to promote this research line by holding the workshop in conjunction with the IJCNLP 2017 conference and also holding the fourth shared task on Chinese Spelling Check. We receive 19 valid submissions for research issues, each of which was reviewed by at least two experts, and have 7 teams participating in the shared task, with 2 of them submitting their testing results. In total, there are 7 oral papers and 5 posters accepted. We also organize a keynote speech in this workshop. The invited speaker Professor Vincent Ng is expected to deliver a great talk entitled as "Towards Content-Based Essay Scoring".

We would like to thank the program committee members for their hard work in completing the review tasks. Their collective efforts achieved quality reviews of the submissions within a few weeks. Great thanks should also go to the speaker, authors, and participants for the tremendous supports in making the workshop a success.

Welcome you to the Taipei city, and wish you enjoy the city as well as the workshop.

NLPTEA 2017 Workshop Chairs
Yuen-Hsien Tseng, National Taiwan Normal University
Hsin-Hsi Chen, National Taiwan University
Lung-Hao Lee, National Taiwan Normal University
Liang-Chih Yu, Yuan Ze University

Organization

Workshop Organizers:

Yuen-Hsien Tseng, National Taiwan Normal University
Hsin-Hsi Chen, National Taiwan University
Lung-Hao Lee, National Taiwan Normal University
Liang-Chih Yu, Yuan Ze University

Shared Task Organizers:

Gabriel Pui Cheong Fung, The Chinese University of Hong Kong
Jia Zhu, South China Normal University

Program Committee:

Yuki Arase, Osaka University
Chris Brockett, Microsoft Research
Christopher Bryant, Cambridge University
Dominique Brunato, National Council of Research, Italy
Lei Chen, Educational Testing Service
Mei-Hua Chen, Tunghai University
Tao Chen, Johns Hopkins University
Vidas Daudaravicius, VTeX Solutions for Science Publishing
Mariano Felice, Cambridge University
Cyril Goutte, National Research Council Canada
Homa B. Hashemi, University of Pittsburgh
Trude Heift, Simon Fraser University, Canada
Tomoyuki Kajiwara, Tokyo Metropolitan University
Mamoru Komachi, Tokyo Metropolitan University
John Lee, City University of Hong Kong
Chen Li, Microsoft
Chuan-Jie Lin, National Taiwan Ocean University
Shervin Malmasi, Harvard University
Tomoya Mizumoto, Tohoku University
Courtney Napoles, John Hopkins University
Simon Ostermann, Saarland University
Arti Ramesh, SUNY - Binghamton University
Gaoqi Rao, Beijing Language and Culture University
Livy Real, IBM Research, Brazil
Alla Rozovskaya, The City University of New York
Elizabeth Salesky, Massachusetts Institute of Technology
Yukio Tono, Tokyo University of Foreign Studies
Elena Volodina, University of Gothenburg
Thuy Vu, University of California, Los Angeles
Shih-Hung Wu, Chaoyang University of Technology
Huichao Xue, Google
Jui-Feng Yeh, National Chiayi University
Zheng Yuan, Cambridge University
Marcos Zampieri, University of Wolverhampton
Torsten Zesch, University of Duisburg-Essen

Invited Talk: Towards Content-Based Essay Scoring

Vincent Ng

Professor of Computer Science
Human Language Technology Research Institute, University of Texas at Dallas

Abstract

State-of-the-art automated essay scoring engines such as E-rater do not grade essay content, focusing instead on providing diagnostic trait feedback on categories such as grammar, usage, mechanics, style and organization. Content-based essay scoring is very challenging: it requires an understanding of essay content and is beyond the reach of today's automated essay scoring technologies. As a result, content-dependent dimensions of essay quality are largely ignored in existing automated essay scoring research. In this talk, we describe our recent and ongoing efforts on content-based essay scoring, sharing the lessons we learned from automatically scoring two of the arguably most important content-dependent dimensions of persuasive essay quality, thesis clarity and argument persuasiveness.

Biography

Vincent Ng (Ph.D., Cornell) is a Professor in the Computer Science Department at the University of Texas at Dallas. He is also the director of the Machine Learning and Language Processing Laboratory in the Human Language Technology Research Institute at UT Dallas. He is currently an associate editor of the ACM Transactions on Asian and Low-Resource Language Information Processing (TALLIP) and an information officer of the ACL Special Interest Group on Chinese Language Processing (SIGHAN). Since 2009, he has become increasingly interested in an NLP application that brings about a number of under-studied but fascinating discourse-level problems, automated essay grading, where he has been focusing on modeling those facets of persuasive student essays that require an understanding of essay content, such as thesis clarity and argument persuasiveness.

Table of Contents

Workshop Program

Friday, December 1, 2017

09:30–09:40   **Opening Remarks**

09:40–10:30   *Towards Content-Based Essay Scoring*
Vincent Ng

10:30–11:00   **Coffee Break**

11:00–12:20   **Regular Paper Session**

11:00–11:20   *NTUCLE: Developing a Corpus of Learner English to Provide Writing Support for Engineering Students*
Roger Vivek Placidus Winder, Joseph MacKinnon, Shu Yun Li, Benedict Christopher Tzer Liang Lin, Carmel Lee Hah Heah, Luís Morgado da Costa, Takayuki Kuribayashi and Francis Bond

11:20–11:40   *Understanding Non-Native Writings: Can a Parser Help?*
Jirka Hana and Barbora Hladka

11:40–12:00   *Carrier Sentence Selection for Fill-in-the-blank Items*
Shu Jiang and John Lee

12:00–12:20   *Hindi Shabdamitra: A Wordnet based E-Learning Tool for Language Learning and Teaching*
Hanumant Redkar, Sandhya Singh, Meenakshi Somasundaram, Dhara Gorasia, Malhar Kulkarni and Pushpak Bhattacharyya

12:20–14:00   **Lunch**

14:00–15:00   **Shared Task Session**

14:00–14:20   *NLPTEA 2017 Shared Task – Chinese Spelling Check*
Gabriel Fung, Maxime Debosschere, Dingmin Wang, Bo Li, Jia Zhu and Kam-Fai Wong

14:20–14:40   *Chinese Spelling Check based on N-gram and String Matching Algorithm*
Jui-Feng Yeh, Li-Ting Chang, Chan-Yi Liu and Tsung-Wei Hsu

14:40–15:00   *N-gram Model for Chinese Grammatical Error Diagnosis*
Jianbo Zhao, Hao Liu, Zuyi Bao, Xiaopeng Bai, Si Li and Zhiqing Lin

15:00–15:20   **Coffee Break**

15:20–15:50   **Poster Session**

The Influence of Spelling Errors on Content Scoring Performance
Andrea Horbach, Yuning Ding and Torsten Zesch

Analyzing the Impact of Spelling Errors on POS-Tagging and Chunking in Learner English
Tomoya Mizumoto and Ryo Nagata

Complex Word Identification: Challenges in Data Annotation and System Performance
Marcos Zampieri, Shervin Malmasi, Gustavo Paetzold and Lucia Specia

Suggesting Sentences for ESL using Kernel Embeddings
Kent Shioda, Mamoru Komachi, Rue Ikeya and Daichi Mochihashi

Event Timeline Generation from History Textbooks
Harsimran Bedi, Sangameshwar Patil, Swapnil Hingmire and Girish Palshikar

NTUCLE: Developing a Corpus of Learner English to Provide Writing Support for Engineering Students

Roger V. P. Winder,♡ Joe MacKinnon,♡ Shu Yun Li,♡ Benedict Lin,♡
Carmel Heah,♡ Luís Morgado da Costa,♠ Takayuki Kuribayashi,♠ and Francis Bond♠
♡Language and Communication Centre, ♠Linguistics and Multilingual Studies
♡♠School of Humanities,
♦Global Asia, Interdisciplinary Graduate School
Nanyang Technological University, Singapore
rogerwinder@ntu.edu.sg

Abstract

This paper describes the creation of a new annotated learner corpus. The aim is to use this corpus to develop an automated system for corrective feedback on students' writing. With this system, students will be able to receive timely feedback on language errors before they submit their assignments for grading. A corpus of assignments submitted by first year engineering students was compiled, and a new error tag set for the NTU Corpus of Learner English (NTUCLE) was developed based on that of the NUS Corpus of Learner English (NUCLE), as well as marking rubrics used at NTU. After a description of the corpus, error tag set and annotation process, the paper presents the results of the annotation exercise as well as follow up actions. The final error tag set, which is significantly larger than that for the NUCLE error categories, is then presented before a brief conclusion summarising our experience and future plans.

1 Introduction

In this paper, we report on a new project which involves the creation of a new annotated Learner Corpus (LC), and which aims to develop an automated system for corrective feedback at Nanyang Technological University (NTU), Singapore. The goal of this system is to provide immediate feedback to students on possible errors in syntax, grammar and lexis, as well as possible style problems, in their assignment drafts.

In this project, we follow studies such as Nagata (1996), which shows that it is not the medium itself (e.g. a computer, a book, a lecturer, etc.) that determines success in learning, it is the quality of the feedback produced by that medium that affects the results. This is why a language teacher is likely to be a better medium than a book, and the same reason why a properly designed Computer Assisted Language Learning (CALL) system can also be a better medium than writing guidelines, assuming that such systems can provide timely and constructive feedback to the learner.

Given our current course design and manpower constraints, students are much more likely to learn from the system's automated feedback than from receiving the same feedback from tutors, which will take longer, after an assignment has been submitted and graded. The immediate feedback through the automated system will enable students to address the possible errors before submitting the final versions for assessment. Consequently, students are more likely to take the feedback seriously because it can be used to improve the quality of the assignment before it is submitted (Price et al., 2010). Furthermore, this automated system will enable tutors to focus more attention on areas that require human judgement in their feedback, such as content, organization and use of rhetorical strategies.

To develop the system, we have tagged an LC of 180 written assignments for a course entitled *Engineering Communication I*, taught at NTU. We then developed an error coding system based on the 27 labels used in the NUS Corpus of Learner English (NUCLE, Dahlmeier et al., 2013) because of similarities in the demographic profile of the participating learners. However, we removed some categories and expanded others so the final list consists of 53 labels. Part of this was to include categories that are not purely grammatical, but pertain to matters of writing style which we are concerned about, some of which can be automatically detected. These include not only obvious style issues such as the use of contractions and collo-

Proceedings of the 4th Workshop on Natural Language Processing Techniques for Educational Applications, pages 1–11,
Taipei, Taiwan, December 1, 2017 ©2017 AFNLP

quial words or expressions but also more subtle ones such as overly long and convoluted sentences and missing parallel clause structures. In this, our corpus distinguishes itself from the Cambridge Learner Corpus (CLC, Nicholls, 2003), NUCLE and other corpora which focus solely on grammar.

Our primary motivation for assembling the NTU Corpus of Learner English (NTUCLE), in other words, is to help individual students to identify their language and style problems, and to rectify these on their own. This is unlike the broader intentions of the CLC, whose error coding and analysis is intended to provide "lexicographers, researchers, ELT [English Language Teaching] authors and examiners with easy, direct information which they can interpret and use for widely varying purposes" (Nicholls, 2003). Similarly, our initial motivation differs from that of the NUCLE, whose goal is to provide a large data resource for research purposes, and for development of grammatical error correction systems (Ng et al., 2014).

Our ultimate goal is also different from many current Natural Language Processing (NLP) projects, which appear to focus on building automated grammatical correction tools, with the holy grail of a "complete end-to-end application" that can identify and correct mistakes for the writers, with a high degree of precision (see Ng et al., 2014). Instead, the goal for NTUCLE was to develop a system that will be able to prompt students to review possible mistakes in their writing drafts and correct them on their own. This will allow learners to participate more meaningfully in the error correction process and to actively identify and choose from multiple options which are often available and would be considered acceptable by different annotators (Rozovskaya and Roth, 2010).

Finally, NTUCLE differs from other similar corpora in its narrower focus on a specific genre (i.e. technical proposals) and target students (i.e. Singaporean engineering undergraduates). Nevertheless, we foresee that our project might be expanded to include other genres and groups of learners, though sub categorisation of specific groups of learners and genres will be ensured.

We have now completed annotation of the corpus, and are currently using this to develop the system for providing feedback to students. This system will detect and tag potential errors in drafts submitted by students, and identify likely errors using our categories. It will not correct any error, but will prompt, with different degrees of confidence, students to consider whether corrections are needed. In this way, we hope to encourage students to adopt a more independent and critical approach to error correction. We also hope to enable a pedagogy focused on timely, high quality feedback to students.

This paper discusses the completed phases of our new LC primarily from the perspective of professional English instructors. In Section 2, we describe the compilation of the corpus and the establishment of initial error tag set. We then describe in Section 3 the annotation process, before presenting in Section 4 the outcomes of our initial annotation, including findings on the most frequent errors identified, inter-annotator differences in tagging and how we resolved them. Section 5 highlights our revised error tag set. We conclude with a brief note on the corpus release, followed by a summary of our experience and our future plans for the corpus.

2 Corpus and Error Tag Set

2.1 Corpus Compilation

Approval was obtained from the university's Institutional Review Board for the research protocol and the use of students' written assignments, subject to the students' consent. Over three semesters (from 2015 to 2016), 349 students gave written consent, and their assignments were retrieved for the corpus.

Of the assignments retrieved, we selected only files in doc/docx format, because it would be difficult to automate text extraction, while preserving headings, paragraphs, style and sentence boundaries for the other formats (e.g. pdf). We ended up with 273 documents from which we tagged only a random sample of 180 documents, due to time and manpower constraints. The 93 untagged documents were kept to test the error-detecting system under development.

The documents are assignments from a communication skills course taught at NTU for first-year engineering students. These authors are predominantly Singaporean (about 80%), with many likely to have native speaker proficiency in English, male (70%), and between 18 and 22 years of age. The assignments consist of a 500-word technical proposal that offers an engineering solution to a real life problem. The solution could be a new product, service or process, or an improvement of an existing one. The instructions for the assignment specify a structure for the proposal consisting of seven sections: background, problem, solution, benefits, implementation, costs/budget and conclusion.

2.2 Initial annotation schema

We next developed a preliminary error tag set by referring to NUCLE (Dahlmeier et al., 2013) as well as marking rubrics used at NTU. Six annotators, all professional English instructors, then tagged the same selected paper from the data set using this tag set. After conferring and reviewing the error tags and agreeing on what constituted an error in the student's paper, we created a modified tag set with 15 broad categories covering 50 error labels. This is much larger than the NUCLE tag set, which has 13 broad categories and 27 error labels, though we were conscious of how excessive granularity could lead to greater difficulty in applying the annotation schema to the documents (Nagata et al., 2011). Below are the ways in which we modified the NUCLE tag set:

Removed two broad categories:

(a) 'Redundancy' because tags created in other categories dealt with this issue more specifically, and

(b) 'Word Choice' replaced with 'Words (lexical)' to reflect a broadening of the category.

Created three additional categories:

(c) 'Expression', covering two tags, 'Awkward expression' (not used in NUCLE) and 'Unclear expression' (similar to 'Unclear meaning' under 'Others' in NUCLE);

(d) 'Prepositions', with three tags (NUCLE covers prepositions under a single tag for 'Wrong collocation/idioms/prepositions'); and

(e) 'Style', with two tags unique to NTUCLE ('StyF' for overly formal words or expressions and 'StySh' for inappropriate shifts in style and formality), and one other tag ('StyC' for inappropriate use of casual or colloquial words or expressions) similar to 'Wtone' for 'Tone' under 'Word Choice' in NUCLE.

Added tags in most categories, through:

(f) specifying whether an error involved something missing, unnecessary or inappropriate (for 'Articles, determiners', 'Prepositions', 'Pronouns', 'Verbs' and 'Words'), similar to the use of 'insertion'/'missing', 'deletion'/'unnecessary' and 'replacement' tags in other projects (see Bryant et al., 2017; Ro-

zovskaya and Roth, 2010);

(g) expanding tags that were collapsed in NUCLE (e.g. two separate tags for run-on sentences and comma splices instead of one, and more specific tags for case, punctuation, spacing and spelling instead of the generic 'Mechanics'); and

(h) creating new tags such as 'VVoice' (for wrong choices of active or passive voice), 'NCount' (for wrong forms of countable/uncountable nouns), and 'SMMod' (for misplaced modifiers) based on errors we have found from experience to be common in our students' writing.

Reduced the error tags in 'Others':

(i) replacing the tag 'Unclear meaning' with the tag 'ExpUC' (for 'Unclear expression') in our new 'Expressions' category.

3 Annotation Process

From the 180 documents collected (see 2.1), each of the 6 annotators was randomly assigned 40 documents, ensuring that 20 of these 40 documents were overlapped evenly with two other annotators (i.e. 10 documents overlapped with another annotator, and another 10 documents overlapped with a second annotator). Each annotator tagged the assigned scripts independently, and the identities of the other annotators tagging the same documents were not revealed. Annotators were also not aware which samples were being double tagged with other annotators. The double tagging was done to check accuracy and inter-annotator agreement.

A total of 60 documents were double annotated. Annotators were instructed to tag every error identified as specifically as possible, and to use more than one tag for the same set of words if there were multiple ways of tagging the error. While we acknowledge that it would also have been useful to correct the errors identified, this was not done because of the complexity of the task, especially in identifying all possible options for correcting each error while preserving the student's intended meaning (Sakaguchi et al., 2017). Unfortunately, this would have required more time and resources than were available.

3.1 Annotation Tool

The annotation process was done on an expanded version of IMI – A Multilingual Semantic Annotation Environment (Bond et al., 2015). We used the open source platform to build an extra layer to the annotation environment, allowing us to tag the documents with our own tag-set (discussed in 2.2 and presented in 5).

The annotators used this new system to tag each document by sentence, in ascending order. Although the system currently only allows tagging sentence by sentence, (i.e. annotators could work on only one sentence at a time on-screen), annotators had access to the full text of each document so that they could identify errors in context (e.g. errors in pronouns with referents in earlier sentences).

To tag each error, annotators could select a single word, a contiguous word-string (e.g. a phrase), a set of non-contiguous words (e.g. a pronoun and its referent earlier or later in the sentence), or the entire sentence. Multiple errors could be tagged for each sentence. Total and partial overlap of errors within the same sentence were allowed and encouraged. This happened, for example, when the same span of words could be corrected in more than one way (i.e. two error tags were assigned to the same span of words), or when a smaller error occurred within a larger error (e.g. an agreement error inside an overly long sentence). Errors were tagged at the level of word tokens, which means that sub-word units could not be selected. Missing words were indicated by tagging the words surrounding the location of the hypothesized missing word. A text-box was provided for each error, which could be used to correct it or to leave comments (e.g. to flag referents that should be anonymized). A screen-shot of the annotation environment is shown in Fig 1.

4 Results and Annotation Issues

The results of the annotation exercise revealed a wide range in the number of errors tagged by each annotator, from 380 (Annotator 2) to 1,183 (Annotator 3), as shown in Table 1. This is not unusual and similar differences have been observed in other annotation exercises (see, for example, Bryant and Ng, 2015). Further discussion suggested that the differences are likely to be due to different levels of sensitivity to particular errors and different tagging practices, including decisions about which particular word, phrase, clause or even sentence to tag with a single label. Annotators also differed in the frequency with which they tagged the same word or word string with different tags to acknowledge different ways of identifying errors. It is also possible, but unlikely, that particular annotators may have received assignments from weaker students – since the assignments were distributed randomly across annotators.

As Table 1 also indicates, three annotators (A2, A3 and A6) were highly similar in their tagging patterns in relation to the three main error categories tagged, namely 'singular/plural forms', 'missing article/determiner' and 'word choice' – which were also the top three error categories overall. Two others (A1 and A5) also had similar top three error categories ('word choice', 'awkward expression' and 'unclear expression') but these were the third, fourth and fifth most common error categories tagged overall.

The five most common errors, distributed by annotators, are shown in Figure 2: errors in using singular or plural forms, omitting articles or determiners, choosing inappropriate words, using awkward expressions and using unclear expressions. However, the annotators appeared to have had different emphases in their annotation. While overall, strictly grammatical errors (i.e. use of singular/plural forms and omission of articles and determiners) were the most commonly identified, annotators 1 and 5 identified far more errors in 'expression' (unclear/awkward), which may relate more to issues in semantics or idiomaticity.

4.1 Double Tagging

As has been mentioned earlier, 60 documents were double tagged. In many cases, both annotators tagged the same errors in the same sentences, either for exactly the same word strings or for word strings with some overlapping words. However, there were also significant differences, such as different word strings tagged for the same error type, or the same word string tagged for different error types.

Interestingly, although two pairs of annotators (A3+A4, and A5+A6) had relatively high degrees of overlap in using the same error tags, they also had relatively high degrees of discrepancy in assigning error tags to the same word strings. This suggests that while they had a strong common understanding of some error tags, they quite possibly also had rather different interpretations of others, or that they had quite different foci where the word strings may have more than one error type.

All the annotators met to review every instance

Figure 1: Annotation tool developed for the corpus annotation, as an extension of IMI

A#	No. Errors	Most Common Error	2nd Most Common Error	3rd Most Common Error
A1	1,101	awkward expression (21%)	word choice (11%)	unclear expression (10%)
A2	380	singular/plural forms (22%)	word choice (7%)	missing article/det. (6%)
A3	1,183	singular/plural forms (12%)	missing article/det. (10%)	word choice (8%)
A4	556	missing article/det. (21%)	singular/plural forms (11%)	verb form (9%)
A5	908	unclear expression (12%)	awkward expression (11%)	word choice (7%)
A6	972	singular/plural forms (11%)	word choice (9%)	missing article/det. (9%)
Total	**5,100**	**singular/plural forms (10%)**	**missing article/det. (8%)**	**word choice (8%)**

Table 1: Top errors by annotator (before harmonisation)

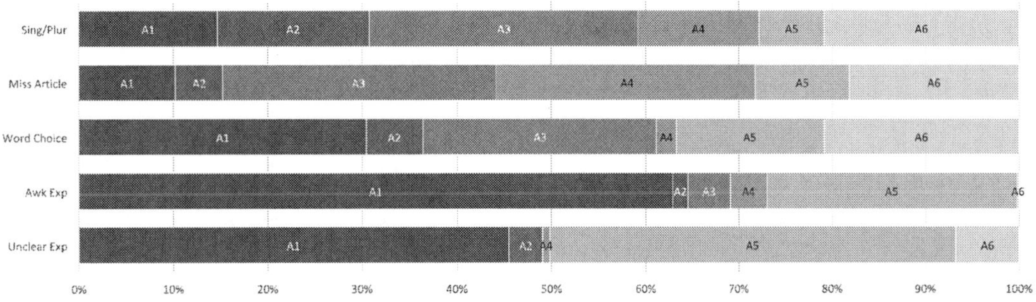

Figure 2: Contributions of annotators to top five errors tagged

of different error tags assigned to the same exact sentence spans (words, expressions, etc.). In most cases, it was agreed that one or both of the annotators had made a mistake, either unintentionally, or through misunderstanding or misapplying a tag. The relevant word strings were then re-tagged with the correct tags. In a few instances, either tag could apply, e.g. *However, trolley has its own limitations*, which can be construed as either 'NNum' (*However, trolleys have their own limitations*) or 'AMiss' (*However, a trolley has its own limitations*). In yet a few others, both tags apply, i.e. there are two errors conflated in the same word set (e.g. *For example, individual seats for individual cubical will be installed with motion sensor.*, where there is both an 'MSpel' (*cubical* to *cubicle*) and 'NNum' (*cubical* to *cubicles*) error). In both these kinds of cases, we agreed that both tags should remain, in the first instance because there are two ways of correcting the error, and in the second, because there are two overlapping errors.

Some differences arose because the annotators involved found it difficult to use existing tags. In many of these instances, one annotator tagged the error under 'Others' and provided his or her own labels or comments. From these, we identified new categories for tagging, namely 'StyMood' for the inappropriate use of imperatives or interrogatives, 'SLong' for overly long sentences, and 'SConv' for convoluted sentences.

We understand that such differences could have been avoided, and the tagging process made more efficient had the annotators been given more detailed guidelines or met for a more extensive standardisation exercise prior to annotation. However, as an exercise to test natural discrepancies in human tagging, this was a useful exercise. Given that our final goal is to emulate human feedback, while providing constructive feedback on issues lecturers usually highlight in student assignments, it was an important part of our experiment to allow this kind of naturalistic tagging, which captures differences in grading expectations, editing experience and perceptions of acceptable or exemplary language use (Daudaravicius et al., 2016; Rozovskaya and Roth, 2010). Consequently, to be able to create a useful error-feedback system, we wanted to restrain ourselves from creating a highly mechanical process to assign tags – even at the cost of inter-annotator agreement.

The annotators also discussed their own 'pet peeves' in the texts they annotated. Among those most commonly shared was the problem of overly long sentences that made comprehension difficult. This reinforced the need for the category 'SLong'. Another commonly shared 'pet peeve' was the inappropriate over-use of certain colloquial words and informal clichés, *tackle* (to mean *study, address* or *solve* a problem) and *hassle* (to mean *inconvenience* or the like) being two of the most common. Another new category 'StyWch' for the use of casual or colloquial words and expressions was created to tag such words.

Our observations of instances tagged for inappropriate style also helped us to identify the specific ways in which this problem was realized in linguistic form, leading to a further two new categories – 'StyContr' for the use of contractions and 'StyPron' for the use of first and second person pronouns.

5 Revised Error Tag Set

The review of the annotation exercise resulted in an amended error tag set with the same 15 categories but with 53 tags. After the amendments, the tag discrepancies mentioned in 4.1 were resolved. Based on the discussion above and the results of the initial tagging, errors that had been tagged under the 'Style' category were re-tagged with one of the tags available in the final tag set.

Table 3 presents our final error tag set, with an indication of the frequency of each error type in the corpus after re-tagging. The 'Source' column indicates how the tags were created:

- 'Sub-divided': broader NUCLE tags that were sub-divided to be more specific
- 'Modified': NUCLE tags that were modified slightly to be more specific
- 'Moved': NUCLE tags that were moved to other categories
- 'NUCLE': NUCLE tags that were not changed
- 'Re-named': NUCLE tags that were re-named to fit the NTUCLE schema
- 'NTUCLE': tags created for NTUCLE

6 Corpus Release

The corpus described above will soon be available at the following url: http://compling.hss.ntu.edu.sg/ntucle.

The corpus includes eight databases, all of them following the database schema used in IMI (Bond et al., 2015). All anonymised data will be released under an Attribution 4.0 International license (CC BY 4.0),[1] in conformity with our IRB and the students' consent.

Table 2 provides a quick overview of the corpus to be released: number of documents, overlaps, number of sentences, number of word tokens, number of sentences that contain at least one error label, and the total number of errors included in each database.

We will release the six individual databases, each tagged by a different professional English instructor, along with a compiled database of the 180 documents tagged, merging documents that were double tagged. While the compiled database has more traditional usages, we believe the individual databases can be used to further analyse and discuss individual differences between annotators. Lastly, we will also release a database with the remaining untagged documents.

7 Conclusion

Based on the NUCLE, we have started the NTU Corpus of Learner English using written assignments submitted by first year engineering students. This corpus will be used to develop an automated system for corrective feedback which is expected to cultivate greater student autonomy and critical awareness in error correction when writing. Our system will be piloted and tested with the next round of submissions for the same writing assignment used to develop the corpus. We plan to add these submissions to the corpus, and keep expanding it.

For our corpus, we have developed a new learner error tag set with 53 tags, which is significantly larger than NUCLE's. This is to meet the specific needs and goals of this corpus, the development of the online tool for corrective feedback without automated correction. As expected, there were significant differences among the annotators in applying the initial tag set, with some annotators being more or less sensitive to particular errors than others. In samples that were double tagged, there were both overlaps and differences in the words tagged and the error tags used. We discussed and resolved all instances where the same word strings were tagged differently, and retagged the word strings. We agreed unanimously that the annotation process could have been im-

proved if more detailed guidelines or brief training had been provided to the annotators prior to annotation. At the same time, the goal of building an automated system for corrective feedback of student's writing, as mentioned above, invited us to firstly acknowledge the low inter-annotator agreement and different foci of professional instructors when correcting student assignments.

We believe that our annotated corpus can be a useful new learner corpus, which can complement and advance on the purposes of corpora such as NUCLE, and we hope to expand it with other genres and learners in the near future. We would like to have the opportunity to further revise and harmonize the annotations in the corpus, and we also acknowledge that it would be beneficial to provide corrections for the identified errors. Unfortunately, this will be dependent on the availability of resources.

All compiled, we are releasing, under an open license, 273 anonymised student assignments, comprising over 14,700 sentences. Roughly 65% of this corpus has been tagged using our newly proposed tagset (available in Table 3).

Acknowledgments

This research is supported by Nanyang Technological University's EdeX Teaching and Learning Grant administered through the Teaching, Learning and Pedagogy Division (TLPD) and the MOE TRF grant *Syntactic Well-Formedness Diagnosis and Error-Based Coaching in Computer Assisted Language Learning using Machine Translation Technology*. We thank the reviewers for their comprehensive comments. We would also like to acknowledge the valuable contributions of Boon Tien Lim in the earlier phases of the project.

References

Francis Bond, Luís Morgado da Costa, and Tuan Anh Le. 2015. IMI – A multilingual semantic annotation environment. In *Proceedings of the 53rd Annual Meeting of the Association for Computational Linguistics and the 7th International Joint Conference on Natural Language Processing of the Asian Federation of Natural Language Processing, System Demonstrations (ACL 2015)*, pages 7–12, Beijing, China.

Christopher Bryant, Mariano Felice, and Ted Briscoe. 2017. Automatic annotation and evaluation of error types for grammatical error correction. In *Proceedings of the 55th Annual Meeting of the Association*

---

[1] https://creativecommons.org/licenses/by/4.0/

DB	Docs.	Overlapped Docs.	Sents.	Words	Sents. w/Errors	Errors
A1	40	10 (A6) + 10 (A2)	2,051	26,176	812	1108
A2	40	10 (A1) + 10 (A3)	2,144	26,764	372	390
A3	40	10 (A2) + 10 (A4)	2,269	27,603	625	1193
A4	40	10 (A3) + 10 (A5)	2,223	27,246	361	575
A5	40	10 (A4) + 10 (A6)	2,093	26,654	579	908
A6	40	10 (A5) + 10 (A1)	2,024	26,103	564	972
Tagged	180	n.a.	9,571	119,727	2,751	4,860
Untagged	93	n.a.	5,174	64,462	n.a.	n.a.
All	273	n.a.	14,745	184,189	n.a.	n.a.

Table 2: Corpus Statistics

for Computational Linguistics, pages 793–805, Vancouver, Canada. Association for Computational Linguistics.

Christopher Bryant and Hwee Tou Ng. 2015. How far are we from fully automatic high quality grammatical error correction? In *Proceedings of the 53rd Annual Meeting of the Association for Computational Linguistics and the 7th International Joint Conference on Natural Language Processing (Volume 1: Long Papers)*, pages 697–707, Beijing, China. Association for Computational Linguistics.

Daniel Dahlmeier, Hwee Tou Ng, and Siew Mei Wu. 2013. Building a large annotated corpus of learner English: The NUS corpus of learner English. In *BEA@ NAACL-HLT*, pages 22–31.

Vidas Daudaravicius, Rafael E. Banchs, Elena Volodina, and Courtney Napoles. 2016. A report on the automatic evaluation of scientific writing shared task. In *Proceedings of the 11th Workshop on Innovative Use of NLP for Building Educational Applications*, pages 53–62, San Diego, CA. Association for Computational Linguistics.

Noriko Nagata. 1996. Computer vs. workbook instruction in second language acquisition. *CALICO journal*, 14(1):53–75.

Ryo Nagata, Edward Whittaker, and Vera Sheinman. 2011. Creating a manually error-tagged and shallow-parsed learner corpus. In *Proceedings of the 49th Annual Meeting of the Association for Computational Linguistics: Human Language Technologies*, pages 1210–1219, Portland, Oregon, USA. Association for Computational Linguistics.

Hwee Tou Ng, Siew Mei Wu, Ted Briscoe, Christian Hadiwinoto, Raymond Hendy Susanto, and Christopher Bryant. 2014. The CoNLL-2014 shared task on grammatical error correction. In *CoNLL Shared Task*, pages 1–14.

Diane Nicholls. 2003. The Cambridge learner corpus: Error coding and analysis for lexicography and elt. In *Proceedings of the Corpus Linguistics 2003 conference*, volume 16, pages 572–581.

Margaret Price, Karen Handley, Jill Millar, and Berry O'Donovan. 2010. Feedback: all that effort, but what is the effect? *Assessment & Evaluation in Higher Education*, 35(3):277–289.

Alla Rozovskaya and Dan Roth. 2010. Annotating esl errors: Challenges and rewards. In *Proceedings of the NAACL HLT 2010 Fifth Workshop on Innovative Use of NLP for Building Educational Applications*, pages 28–36, Los Angeles, California. Association for Computational Linguistics.

Keisuke Sakaguchi, Courtney Napoles, and Joel Tetreault. 2017. Gec into the future: Where are we going and how do we get there? In *Proceedings of the 12th Workshop on Innovative Use of NLP for Building Educational Applications*, pages 180–187, Copenhagen, Denmark. Association for Computational Linguistics.

Categories	Tags	Explanation	Freq.	Source
Articles, determiners	ACh	Wrong choice of article/determiner *A development of a new product is required*	69	Expanded
	AMiss	Missing article/determiner *a stall with [a] shorter queue*	449	Expanded
	AUnn	Unnecessary article/determiner *two holes in the two of the sides*	144	Expanded
Citations	CitForm	Incorrect citation form *(Sim, R. 2013)*	100	Expanded
	CitMiss	Missing citation *According to a study [citation], Singaporean students …*	6	Expanded
Expression	ExpAw	Awkward expression (meaning is clear) *paths are of high human traffic*	366	NTUCLE
	ExpUC	Unclear expression (meaning is unclear) *A rubbish bin to test our idea as well as human resources from the companies*	249	Moved
Mechanics	MCase	Wrong use of upper or lower case *The Rubbish bin is a common object*	98	Expanded
	MPunc	Punctuation error *This[,] in turn[,] would create an orderly environment*	190	Expanded
	MSpace	Missing or unnecessary space *They can not be used in open areas*	27	Expanded
	MSpel	Spelling error *a cold and quite environment*	58	Expanded
Nouns	NCount	Wrong form of countable/uncountable noun *Users can exchange notes and advices*	77	NTUCLE
	NNum	Wrong choice of singular/plural form of the noun *one of his speech*	525	NUCLE
	NPoss	Wrong choice of possessive form *the timers can be adjusted to workers['] feedback*	22	NUCLE
Prepositions	PreCh	Wrong choice of preposition *at the comfort of his home*	227	Expanded
	PreMiss	Missing preposition *EasyGrip will be a great addition [to] every household*	53	Expanded
	PreUnn	Unnecessary preposition *video tutorials can be played to teach users on how to use the mouse*	54	Expanded
Pronouns	ProAgr	Pronoun and reference do not agree in number/person/gender *An electrostatic precipitator works by absorbing dirty air, passing them through ionising electrodes*	88	Re-named
	ProCh	Wrong choice of pronoun *they things tend to slip off their mind easily*	32	Expanded
	ProMiss	Missing pronoun *5 'X's will identify owners as irresponsible and deny [them] a pet.*	21	Expanded
	ProRef	Unclear reference for pronoun *The components can be mounted onto a circuit board, which is covered with a plastic housing once it is completed.*	92	Modified
	ProUnn	Unnecessary pronoun *Death then follows if the victim he is been left untreated within minutes*	8	Expanded

Categories	Tags	Explanation	Freq.	Source
Sentence structure	SComS	Comma splice	40	Expanded
		The wobbling table can cause food and drinks to be spilled out of their containers, writing can become messy.		
	SConv	Convoluted sentence	-	NTUCLE
		Rubbish bins are facing one problem in crowded areas where bins fill up quickly that cleaners have hard time discerning as there are too many bins, and only come at fixed timings to clear the rubbish currently.		
	SDMod	Dangling modifier	16	Expanded
		Looking at the bigger picture, a canteen can efficiently accommodate more diners in a given time.		
	SFrag	Sentence fragment	58	NUCLE
		Thus, showing that our students have a huge desire to always learn something new.		
	SLong	Overly long sentence	14	NTUCLE
		However, they would not be able to do the required printing if they possess an EZ-link card that has insufficient stored monetary value and hence may require the assistance of friends by borrowing their EZ-link cards, or make their way back to (...) [+38 words]		
	SMMod	Misplaced modifier	11	NTUCLE
		An ideal conducive learning environment is essential as it facilitates effective teaching and learning process coupled with a well-equipped lecture theatre		
	SPar	Parallelism missing	37	NUCLE
		students will find it a hassle to go through emails and calling to find out more		
	SRun	Run-on sentence	26	Expanded
		there is an increase in commuters for public transport[;] this leads to higher congestion in public transport		
	SSub	Problematic subordinate clause	25	NUCLE
		The immediate benefited [sic] ones would be the needy groups, directly solving their food shortage.		
Style	StyContr	Contractions	25	NTUCLE
		It's a rectangular device		
	StyF	Overly formal words or expressions	1	NTUCLE
		To solve the aforementioned problems		
	StyMood	Inappropriate use of interrogatives and imperatives	13	NTUCLE
		Establish a collaboration with an existing music-streaming app.		
	StyPron	Inappropriate use of first and second person pronouns	9	NTUCLE
		I could not manage to find the cost of one EZ link top up machine		
	StyWch	Casual or colloquial words or expressions	92	NTUCLE
		some find it a hassle to search for an available power socket		
Subject-verb agreement	SubVA	Subject and verb do not agree in number and/or person	148	NUCLE
		The portable charger are basically portable		

Categories	Tags	Explanation	Freq.	Source
Transitions	TCh	Wrong choice of link words/phrases *Hence users will also be able to purchase a UV light, <u>where</u> they can use it to identify areas which were not cleaned properly*	50	Expanded
	TMiss	Missing link words/phrases *The food owners select the nearest food <u>centre, [and] fill</u> in their address and contact number.*	26	Expanded
	TUnn	Unnecessary link words/phrases *Skipping lunch can cause students to be distracted by hunger <u>and</u> thus affecting academic performance.*	34	Expanded
Verbs	VForm	Wrong form of the verb *NTU is <u>rank</u> 13th in the world*	231	NUCLE
	VMiss	Missing verb *The files they <u>need [?] directly</u> streamed to their computer.*	23	NUCLE
	VMod	Missing, inappropriate or unnecessary modal *To produce the application, the following steps <u>are</u> taken:*	138	NUCLE
	VTense	Verb tense *Each year Nanyang Technological University (NTU) <u>welcomed</u> approximately 4,500 students into their freshmen year*	121	NUCLE
	VVoice	Wrong choice of active or passive voice *The phenomenon of overcrowding of Canteen B <u>has been existed</u> for a long time.*	27	NTUCLE
Word order	PosAd	Wrong position of adjective/adverb *vacuum cleaners can be used to clean narrow spaces <u>also</u>*	3	Re-named
	PosW	Incorrect word order *the problem of <u>dropping things off</u> the desk*	13	Re-named
Words (lexical)	WCh	Wrong choice of word *The air conditioner is an electric appliance that <u>alternates</u> the surrounding temperature.*	411	NTUCLE
	WColloc	Words do not collocate *<u>Find assistance from</u> Sistic to sell tickets*	73	NTUCLE
	WForm	Wrong form of the word *Rentascoot™ is <u>environmental</u> friendly*	96	NUCLE
	WMiss	Missing words *This system can <u>simplify [?] and</u> reduce the time of packing <u>away [?]</u>.*	95	NTUCLE
	WUnn	Unnecessary words *... which poses severe risks to nature as well as human health <u>issues</u>*	195	NTUCLE
Others	Oth	Other errors requiring correction	140	NUCLE

Table 3: Final list of error tags. Examples for each error are provided below the explanation of each tag, with the words selected for each error underlined. Possible corrections are provided in brackets when deemed necessary.

Parsing Writings of Non-Native Czech

Jirka Hana and **Barbora Hladká**
Charles University
Malostranské nám. 25
118 00 Prague 1
Czech Republic
{hana, hladka}@ufal.mff.cuni.cz

Abstract

We present a pilot study on parsing
non-native texts written by learners of
Czech. We performed experiments that
have shown that at least high-level syntactic functions, like subject, predicate, and
object, can be assigned based on a parser
trained on standard native language.

1 Introduction

Texts written by non-native speakers pose a challenge for natural language processing. In this paper, we focus on parsing texts written by learners
of Czech. There is no syntactically annotated corpus of non-native Czech. Therefore, we are exploring a question whether it is possible to use the
parser trained a traditional newspaper corpus.

In our experiments we use three main components: the *Prague Dependency Treebank*, the
CzeSL corpus, and the *maximum-spanning tree
parser*.

The *Prague Dependency Treebank* (PDT) [1] is a
corpus of newspaper texts with rich linguistic annotation. As an illustration, consider the sentence
in (1) and the corresponding labeled dependency
tree in Figure 1:

(1) Ráno   půjdu   se   svým
    in-the-morning I-will-go with my
    kamarádem na houby.
    friend   mushrooming.
    'I will go mushrooming with my friend in
    the morning.'

The *CzeSL* corpus includes essays written
by non-native speakers of Czech (Rosen et al.,
2013). Finally, the *maximum-spanning tree (MST)
parser* is a non-projective dependency parser that

---

[1] https://ufal.mff.cuni.cz/pdt3.0

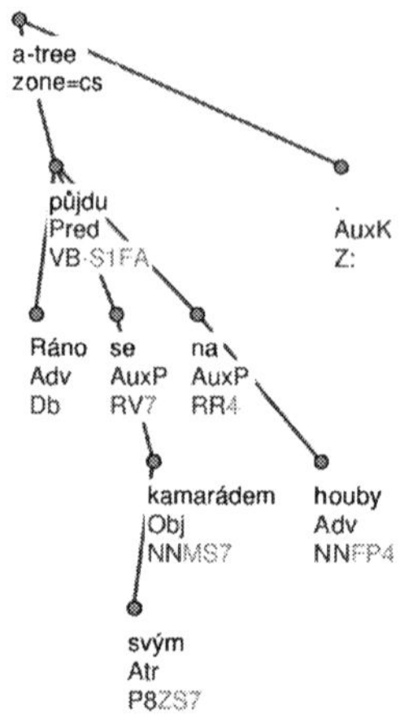

Figure 1: A sample of PDT tree

searches for maximum spanning trees over di-
rected graphs (McDonald et al., 2005).

Given these data and tool components we specify the following initial steps to address our research question:

1. Create a testing corpus, by annotating CzeSL
   according to the PDT annotation guidelines

2. Parse CzeSL by the MST parser trained on
   PDT or its subset and evaluate its performance

2 Related work

Research on parsing has mostly concentrated on
parsing the traditional treebanks. Therefore most
parsers have statistical models that are optimized
for the syntactic annotations in these treebanks and
more generally for their language. This means that
such parsers will show a degradation in performance when used for parsing data from another
domain. Thus research has started on adapting
parsers to new domains. One of the first venues

Proceedings of the 4th Workshop on Natural Language Processing Techniques for Educational Applications, pages 12–16,
Taipei, Taiwan, December 1, 2017 ©2017 AFNLP

at which domain adaptation was targeted was the 2007 CoNLL shared task on dependency parsing, see (Nivre et al., 2007).

One of the challenges in domain adaptation for parsing is the lack of annotated data in the target domain that could be used for evaluation. Focusing on the domain of learner texts and their parsing, the great majority of works concern texts of English learners. We support this fact with a list of learner corpora in Table 1 where their basic characteristics are provided.

Dickinson and Ragheb (2015) consider very carefully the SALLE annotation scheme for syntactically annotating learner English.[2] Napoles et al. (2016) studied the effect of grammatical errors on the dependency parse. As the source of the data, they used the NUCLE corpus. Berzak et al. (2016) benchmarked POS tagging and dependency parsing performance on the TLE dataset and measure the effect of grammatical errors on parsing accuracy. Cahill et al. (2014) used self-training parsing technique with both native and non-native training texts. They found that both training sets performed at about the same level, but that both significantly outperformed the baseline parser trained on traditional labeled data.

3 Syntactic annotation of CzeSL

The *CzeSL* corpus includes transcriptions of essays written by non-native speakers of Czech. It is focused on native speakers of three main language groups: Slavic, other Indo-European, and non-Indo-European. The hand-written texts cover all language levels, from real beginners to advanced learners.

In this paper, the CzeSL corpus refers to the *CzeSL-man* corpus that consists of 645 texts written by 262 different authors who are native speakers of 32 different languages. As shown in Table 2, the texts belong mostly to A2-B2 CEFR.[3]

Its annotation scheme consists of three interconnected layers:

- the T0 layer contains anonymised transcripts of the originals,

- the T1 layer corrects non-existing word forms ignoring context,

---

[2]http://cl.indiana.edu/~salle/

[3]The Common European Framework of Reference for Languages; see https://en.wikipedia.org/wiki/Common_European_Framework_of_Reference_for_Languages.

Level	Documents	Level	Documents
A1	57	B1	176
A1+	3	B2	124
A2	111	C1	12
A2+	145	Unknown	17

Table 2: Composition of CzeSL according to CEFR levels.

Jmenujese Adam. Ja jsem Mongolska. Mongolska ma 21 kraji. Moje rodina je hezka ješte velka. Mongolska je 3000 million lidi. Ma tradični píseňka, taneční. Mongolska tradični písenka je hezka. Ješte ma "Morin khuur". Morin Khuur to je muzika. Ten hezka tradični pohádka, píseň. Mongolska má mnoho tradiční svátík. Třiba Naadam, Tsagaarsur. Ješte mnoho Velbloud, Kůn, Kravá, Koza, Ovce. Mongolsky lidi dobrý. Mongolsko ma mnoho horý a nemam ocean. Mongolska hlavní náměsto. Ulaanbaatar. ADAM, 18 Let Bydlim v Čechagh už 6 měsíc. 1. AHOJ

Figure 2: An essay written by a 16+ male student of the non Indo-European language group staying in the Czech Republic less than a year. The essay is on My family.

- the T2 layer corrects all other types of errors, including syntactic errors.

In our experiment, we focus on learner language, therefore we use only the T0 layer, disregarding any corrections made on the T1 and T2 layers.

Learner texts typically differ from newspaper corpora, i.e., highly edited texts written by native speakers, in two aspects: first, they contain errors in spelling, grammar, vocabulary, and collocations; second, they have a different distribution of vocabulary and syntactic constructions.

For illustration, consider a sample essay in Table 2. The text is perfectly understandable, yet it contains errors practically in every sentence and about every other word. Some of these deviations from native language make annotation with traditional grammatical categories quite complicated. For example, consider the second sentence: *Ja jsem Mongolska* meaning 'I am Mongolian' or 'I

	TLE	**NUCLE**	**SALLE**	**CzeSL**
	Berzak et al. (2016)	Dahlmeier et al. (2013)	Dickinson and Ragheb (2013)	Rosen et al. (2013)
L2	English	English	English	Czech
entity	corpus	corpus	framework	corpus
volume	5,124 sentences	1,414 texts	NA	645 texts
error annotation	●	●	NA	●
POS tags	●	○	NA	○
Universal Dependencies	●	○	NA	○

Table 1: A number of learner corpora (● annotation present, ○ annotation not-present, Not Applicable).

am from Mongolia'. The non-existent word *Mongolska* can be interpreted in at least the following three ways:

1. it is an adjective (*mongolská* or *mongolský*) and thus syntactically a predicative nominal;

2. it is a name of an inhabitant (*Mongol*), a noun, syntactically a predicative nominal;

3. a place (*z Mongolska*), a noun, syntactically an adverbial (adjunct).

It is not clear, whether the language of the speaker actually distinguishes all of these categories.

Learner language is challenging not just for NLP tools, but for human annotation as well. We decided to start partial syntactic analysis. Instead of building a complete dependency tree and labelling each node, we opted to perform a linear annotation of subjects, objects, predicates and predicative nominals.

Two high-level annotation instructions were formulated:

1. Use the PDT guidelines[4] to mark subjects, objects, predicates and nominals with the corresponding PDT syntactic functions `Sb`, `Obj`, `Pred`, `Pnom`, resp.

2. Annotate the language of the learner, not the target hypothesis (a standard Czech expression with the same meaning). For example, if the learner uses the phrase (2), the word *místnost* 'room' is annotated as an object, even though a native speaker would use an adverbial *do místnosti* 'into room'.

   (2) vstoupit místnost
           enter   room   .
       'intended: enter a room.'

   (3) vstoupit do   místnosti
           enter   into room   .
       'enter a room.'

In this, we are consistent with other annotation projects, for example the SALLE project: *Try to assume as little as possible about the intended meaning of the learner.* (Dickinson and Ragheb, 2013)

Unlike a traditional treebanking project, which is a very expensive activity, the CzeSL corpus was annotated in three months by one annotator with a philological education. Instead of intensive training, the annotator annotated the data and studied the guidelines in parallel. When she was in doubt, she consulted the problem with an experienced linguist who annotated the Prague Dependency Treebank. The annotator used the Brat editor.[5]

4 Experiments

We experimented with two different parsers: (i) a traditional parser trained on PDT (ii) a parser trained on a simpler subset of Czech. In both cases, we used the MST parser.

4.1 STYX – Training on simpler language

On average, sentences in newspapers have a more complicated structure than sentences found in a typical non-native text. This motivated us to experiment with a parser that would be trained on a corpus using simpler syntax than that of PDT.

Hladká and Kučera (2008) present the STYX, an electronic corpus-based exercise book of Czech grammar.[6] The STYX corpus is based on PDT, but contains only "simple" sentences.

---

[4]`https://ufal.mff.cuni.cz/pdt2.0/doc/manuals/en/a-layer/pdf/a-man-en.pdf`

[5]`http://brat.nlplab.org/`
[6]`http://hdl.handle.net/11234/1-2391`

syntactic function	P	R	F1	# tokens in the test data
1. parser: MST_{PDT}			test data: CzeSL	
Pred	0.87	0.80	0.83	13,762
Sb	0.60	0.37	0.46	8,119
Obj	0.44	0.61	0.51	12,615
Pnom	0.38	0.50	0.43	2,870
avg / total	0.63	0.62	0.61	37,366
2. parser: MST_{Styx}			test data: CzeSL	
Pred	0.70	0.83	0.76	13,762
Sb	0.41	0.31	0.35	8,119
Obj	0.51	0.50	0.51	12,615
Pnom	0.40	0.23	0.29	2,870
avg / total	0.55	0.56	0.55	37,366
3. parser: MST_{PDT}			test data: Styx_{etest}	
Pred	0.99	0.98	0.98	1,220
Sb	0.58	0.34	0.42	1,059
Obj	0.34	0.60	0.43	1,066
Pnom	0.37	0.52	0.43	198
avg / total	0.64	0.65	0.62	3,543
4. parser: MST_{Styx}			test data: Styx_{etest}	
Pred	0.95	0.96	0.95	1,220
Sb	0.62	0.37	0.47	1,059
Obj	0.58	0.49	0.53	1,066
Pnom	0.49	0.34	0.40	198
avg / total	0.71	0.61	0.65	3,543

Table 3: We measure the performance of the MST parser using the following performance measures: Precision, Recall, and F1 measure.

4.2 Results

We have evaluated the two parsers against the manual annotation of CzeSL. For comparison, we have also evaluated them on Styx, i.e. a corpus of native Czech. The results are summarized in Table 3. The subscript indicates which corpus was used for training (MST_{PDT} vs MST_{Styx}). The results are surprising in two ways:

1. the performance on the learner language is nearly comparable to the performance on native Czech.

2. training the parser on a simpler language not only does not help, but actually hurts the performance

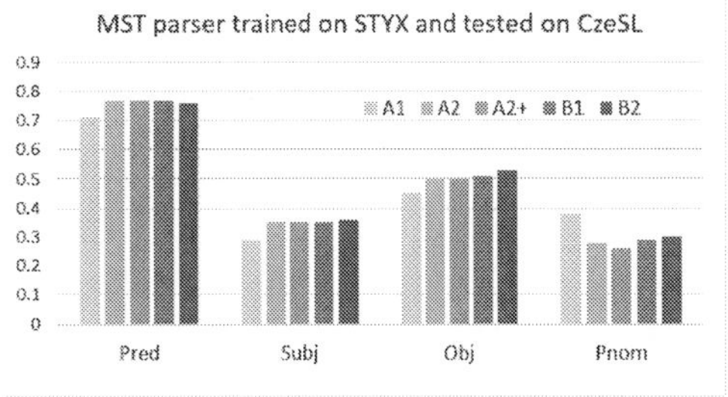

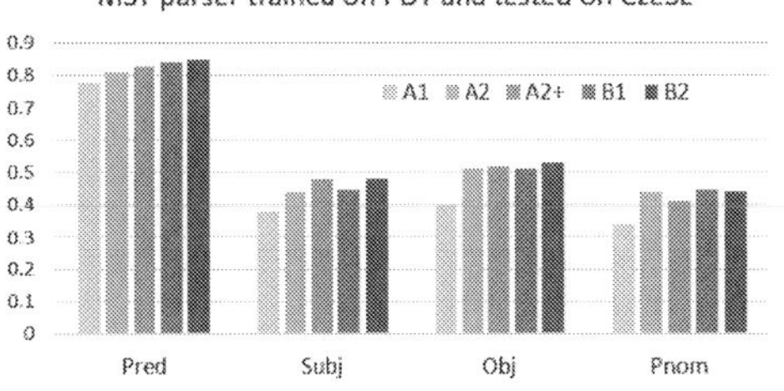

Figure 3: Performance of the parsers on CzeSL: F1-measure CEFR levels. (A1+ and C1 are omitted due to low number of documents)

Figure 3 shows performance of the parsers on the CzeSL corpus by syntactic category and CEFR level. For the PDT parser, the performance is worst for A1 and better on more advanced levels, as expected. However, starting with A2+ level, the performance does not improve with CEFR levels. One of the explanations might be that on the one hand those advanced texts contain less "low-level" errors (errors in spelling and morphology), but on the other hand the sentences get longer and get a more complicated syntax structure.

5 Conclusion and future work

Our experiments have shown that at least high-level syntactic functions, non-native text can be assigned based on a parser trained on standard native language. It has also shown, that training the parser on a subset of standard language limited to simpler construction provided no benefit. Currently, we focus on two main tasks:

- Repeating the annotation of a part of the CzeSL corpus with a second annotator, to be able to calculate inter-annotator agreement

- Evaluating the possibility of annotating additional syntactic functions and possibly a limited structure

Acknowledgments

We gratefully acknowledge support from the Grant Agency of the Czech Republic, grant No. ID 16-10185S.

References

Yevgeni Berzak, Jessica Kenney, Carolyn Spadine, Jing Xian Wang, Lucia Lam, Keiko Sophie Mori, Sebastian Garza, and Boris Katz. 2016. Universal Dependencies for Learner English. *CoRR*, abs/1605.04278.

Aoife Cahill, Binod Gyawali, and James Bruno. 2014. Self-training for parsing learner text. In *Proceedings of the First Joint Workshop on Statistical Parsing of Morphologically Rich Languages and Syntactic Analysis of Non-Canonical Languages*, pages 66–73, Dublin, Ireland. Dublin City University.

Daniel Dahlmeier, Hwee Tou Ng, and Siew Mei Wu. 2013. Building a large annotated corpus of learner english: The nus corpus of learner english. In *Proceedings of the Eighth Workshop on Innovative Use of NLP for Building Educational Applications*, pages 22–31, Atlanta, Georgia. Association for Computational Linguistics.

Markus Dickinson and Marwa Ragheb. 2013. Annotation for learner english guidelines, v. 0.1 (june 2013).

Markus Dickinson and Marwa Ragheb. 2015. On Grammaticality in the Syntactic Annotation of Learner Language. In *Proceedings of The 9th Linguistic Annotation Workshop*, pages 158–167, Denver, CO.

Barbora Hladká and Ondřej Kučera. 2008. An annotated corpus outside its original context: A corpus-based exercise book. In *ACL 2008: Proceedings of the Third Workshop on Innovative Use of NLP for Building Educational Applications*, pages 36–43, Columbus, OH, USA. Association for Computational Linguistics (ACL).

Ryan McDonald, Fernando Pereira, Kiril Ribarov, and Jan Hajič. 2005. Non-projective dependency parsing using spanning tree algorithms. In *Proceedings of the Conference on Human Language Technology and Empirical Methods in Natural Language Processing*, HLT '05, pages 523–530, Stroudsburg, PA, USA. Association for Computational Linguistics.

Courtney Napoles, Aoife Cahill, and Nitin Madnani. 2016. The effect of multiple grammatical errors on processing non-native writing. In *Proceedings of the 11th Workshop on Innovative Use of NLP for Building Educational Applications*, pages 1–11, San Diego, CA. Association for Computational Linguistics.

Joakim Nivre, Johan Hall, Sandra Kübler, Ryan McDonald, Jens Nilsson, Sebastian Riedel, and Deniz Yuret. 2007. The conll 2007 shared task on dependency parsing. In *Proceedings of the CoNLL Shared Task Session of EMNLP-CoNLL 2007*, pages 915–932, Prague, Czech Republic. Association for Computational Linguistics.

Alexandr Rosen, Jirka Hana, Barbora Štindlová, and Anna Feldman. 2013. Evaluating and automating the annotation of a learner corpus. *Language Resources and Evaluation*, pages 1–28.

Carrier Sentence Selection for Fill-in-the-blank Items

Shu Jiang
Department of
Computer Science and Engineering
Shanghai Jiao Tong University
Shanghai, China
jshmjs45@gmail.com

John Lee
Department of
Linguistics and Translation
City University of Hong Kong
Hong Kong SAR, China
jsylee@cityu.edu.hk

Abstract

Fill-in-the-blank items are a common form of exercise in computer-assisted language learning systems. To automatically generate an effective item, the system must be able to select a high-quality carrier sentence that illustrates the usage of the target word. Previous approaches for carrier sentence selection have considered sentence length, vocabulary difficulty, the position of the target word and the presence of finite verbs. This paper investigates the utility of word co-occurrence statistics and lexical similarity as selection criteria. In an evaluation on generating fill-in-the-blank items for learning Chinese as a foreign language, we show that these two criteria can improve carrier sentence quality.

1 Introduction

Fill-in-the-blank items are a common form of exercise in computer-assisted language learning (CALL) systems. Also known as cloze or gap-fill items, they are constructed on the basis of *carrier sentences*. One word in the carrier sentence — called the *target word*, or the "key" — is blanked out. The learner attempts to fill in this blank, sometimes with the help of several choices, which include the target word itself and several distractors. Consider the following item, in Chinese, for the target word *xiande* 顯得 'appear, seem, look':

與其他生物相比，人類的生產過程
___ 複雜許多。

Compared with other organisms, the human reproductive process ___ a lot more complex.

(A) *xiande* 顯得 'appear, seem, look'
(B) ... (C) ... (D) ...

This carrier sentence not only makes a point about the human reproductive process, but also illustrates a typical usage of *xiande* by providing a comparison. In contrast, the following carrier sentence is an inferior choice for illustrating the same target word. Though perfectly fluent and grammatical, it does not offer any reason or context for the appearance of the pilot:

他回到駕駛艙，臉色 ___ 蒼白。

He returned to the cockpit, and his face ___ pale.

Authoring fill-in-the-blank items, and composing carrier sentences in particular, is labor-intensive. There has thus been much interest in automatic generation of these items for self-directed language learners. Previous research on fill-in-the-blank item generation has mostly focused on finding plausible distractors. In the only published studies on carrier sentence selection (Volodina et al., 2012; Pilán et al., 2013), the system makes the selection based on sentence length, vocabulary difficulty, the position of the target word, and the presence of finite verbs. We show that two additional criteria — word co-occurrence and lexical similarity, which take into account the relation between the target word and other words in the carrier sentence — can improve the quality of the selected carrier sentence.

2 Previous work

This section summarizes previous work on carrier sentence selection (Section 2.1), supplemented by two related research areas: example sentence selection for dictionaries (Section 2.2), and text readability prediction (Section 2.3).

Proceedings of the 4th Workshop on Natural Language Processing Techniques for Educational Applications, pages 17–22,
Taipei, Taiwan, December 1, 2017 ©2017 AFNLP

2.1 Carrier sentence selection

Automatic generation of fill-in-the-blank items requires selection of distractors and carrier sentences. Previous research mostly focused on the former (Liu et al., 2005; Sumita et al., 2005; Chen et al., 2006; Smith et al., 2010; Sakaguchi et al., 2013; Zesch and Melamud, 2014). As for carrier sentences, some systems use example sentences from dictionaries (Pino and Eskenazi, 2009), while others impose relatively simple requirements (Meurers et al., 2010; Knoop and Wilske, 2013).

We are not aware of any reported work on carrier sentence selection for Chinese. To the best of our knowledge, apart from general guidelines (Haladyna et al., 2002; Xu, 2012), the only work on sentence selection for language-learning exercises focused on Swedish. Volodina et al. (2012) proposed an algorithm that uses four weighted heuristics — sentence length, position of the target word, absence of rare words and presence of finite verbs — to score each candidate sentence. In manual evaluation, 56.6% of the sentences were considered "acceptable". In a subsequent evaluation on the *Lärka* system (Pilán et al., 2013), human judges rated 73% of the automatically selected sentences to be "understandable"; they rated about 60% as suitable as exercise items or as examples for vocabulary illustration.

2.2 Example sentence selection

A dictionary entry of a word often includes an example sentence. Various criteria for selecting an example sentence for dictionaries have been proposed (Kilgarriff et al., 2008; Didakowski et al., 2012). As far as the sentence is concerned, it must be authentic, complete, well-formed, self-contained, and not too complex. As for the target word, it should not be used as a proper noun, or in a metaphoric or abstract sense; further, it should co-occur often with, and be semantically related to, one or more words in the rest of the sentence. A number of systems have implemented some of these criteria as heuristic rules (Smith et al., 2009; Baisa and Suchomel, 2014). In one study, these criteria yielded 95% success rate in example sentence selection (Didakowski et al., 2012). Since a carrier sentence should likewise illustrate the usage of its target word, we will borrow some of these criteria — specifically, word co-occurrence and lexical similarity — in this work.

2.3 Text readability prediction

Text readability prediction classifies a document into a difficulty level, typically a school grade. State-of-the-art systems combine lexical, syntactic and discourse features, as well as n-gram language model scores, to perform the classification (Schwarm and Ostendorf, 2005; Pitler and Nenkova, 2008; Kate et al., 2010; Collins-Thompson, 2008).

For Chinese, we are aware of only two reported studies on this task. Using similar features as above, Sung et al. (2015) achieved 72.92% accuracy in classifying textbook material into the six grades at primary school. Chen et al. (2013) showed that tf-idf and lexical chains can further improve accuracy, ranging from 80% to 96% for various grade levels on a set of textbooks.

Although carrier sentences must also be highly readable, features used in text readability prediction are not directly transferrable to our task. Most of these features are intended for documents, and may not work well when applied on single sentences. In a recent study on sentence-level readability prediction for Swedish, Pilán et al. (2014) found that a heuristic approach based on example sentence selection (Kilgarriff et al., 2008) outperformed a statistical classifier that adapts features from document-level readability prediction.

3 Features for carrier sentence selection

Because of the lack of large-scale, annotated dataset for carrier sentence selection, it is impossible to use standard machine learning methods for scoring candidate carrier sentences. Instead, we developed a number of features, to be used by the system as heuristics. We first describe baseline features (Section 3.1) inspired by Volodina et al. (2012), and then investigate word co-occurrence and lexical similarity statistics (Section 3.2).

To tune the heuristics, we compiled two datasets. The "Textbook Set" consists of 299 carrier sentences, drawn from fill-in-the-blank questions in three Chinese textbooks (Liu, 2004, 2010; Wang, 2007)[1]. The "Wiki Set" contains 9.2 million sentences, harvested from Chinese Wikipedia. We performed word segmentation, part-of-speech tagging and syntactic parsing with the Stanford Chinese parser (Levy and Manning, 2003).

---

[1] We excluded carrier sentences whose target words are not nouns, verbs, or adjectives.

3.1 Baseline features

Sentence complexity. In fill-in-the-blank items intended for self-directed learning, as opposed to assessment, simple sentences are preferred. This is to minimize the learner's difficulties in sentence comprehension and optimize his/her acquisition of the target word. An indicator of sentence complexity is sentence length; for example, Volodina et al. (2012) favor sentences between 10 and 15 words. The average length of carrier sentences in the Textbook Set is 16.8 words, substantially shorter than that of sentences in the Wiki Set (24.7 words). Besides sentence length, the number of clauses can also serve as an approximate measure of complexity. On average, the parse tree of a carrier sentence in the textbooks contains 3.1 IP nodes[2]. *We require a carrier sentence to have between 10 to 20 words, and to have no more than 3 IP nodes.*

Vocabulary difficulty. For similar reasons as described above, carrier sentences tend to avoid difficult words. Word frequency is often used as a proxy for its difficulty level. While a straightforward strategy is to set a minimum frequency threshold (Volodina et al., 2012), no fixed threshold can suit all individual learners, and a conservative threshold would unnecessarily reject good candidate sentences. We instead take the target word as the point of reference — a carrier sentence designed for teaching that word should not assume the learner to know words that are more advanced. We ranked all words by frequency in the Wiki Set, and divide them into buckets of 1,000 words. *We require all words in the carrier sentence to belong to the same bucket as, or a higher word-frequency bucket than, the target word.*

Target word position. While Volodina et al. (2012) prefer target words to be located within the first 10 words of the sentence, the target words in the Textbook Set tend to occur in the second half of the sentence, and fewer than 1% are within the first tenth of the sentence.[3] *We require that the target word cannot be situated within the first tenth of the carrier sentence.*

Complete sentence. To favor complete sentences, the heuristic used by Volodina et al. (2012) rewards the presence of a finite verb. Since Chinese verbs do not mark finiteness, we instead require a carrier sentence to have a subject. The subject of a sentence is often dropped in Chinese, a pro-drop language. Although such a sentence is perfectly grammatical, it is undesirable as a carrier sentence since it cannot be interpretable in isolation. *We require the root of the carrier sentence to have a noun subject.*[4]

3.2 Target word features

Word Co-occurrence. A good sentence "should present words with which [the target word] typically co-occurs" (Didakowski et al., 2012). We measure co-occurrence with pointwise mutual information (PMI), estimated on the Wiki Set. We compute the "PMI Score" of a sentence by finding the word in the sentence that has the highest PMI with the target word. Table 1 shows the carrier sentence with the maximum PMI score for the target word *xiande* 'appear, seem, look'. The word that yields the highest PMI with the target word is *xiangbi* 'compare', reflecting a typical use of *xiangbi* to introduce a second element ("other organisms") to contrast with the subject ("human"). *We select the carrier sentence with the highest PMI Score with respect to the target word.*

Lexical similarity. A good sentence should "contain words that are lexically-semantically related to [the target word]" (Didakowski et al., 2012). We trained a continuous bag of words (CBOW) model of 400 dimensions and window size 5 with word2vec (Mikolov et al., 2013) on the Wiki Set. We computed the "Similarity Score" of a sentence by finding the word in the sentence that has the highest word2vec similarity score with the target word[5]. Table 1 shows the carrier sentence with the maximum similarity score for the target word *xiande* 'appear, seem, look'. The word that yields the highest similarity score with the target word is *gengwei* 'even more', a verb that is often used in similar context. *We select the carrier sentence with the highest Similarity Score with respect to the target word.*

4 Experiment set-up

Among the target words in fill-in-the-blank items in the Textbook Set, we selected 100 words — 56 verbs, 31 nouns and 13 adjectives — such

---

[2]An IP node corresponds to an S or SBAR node in the Penn Treebank.

[3]More precisely, the average target word position is 7.1 out of a ten-word sentence. The optimal word position might differ by language, and deserves further investigation.

[4]That is, the root, typically a verb, a noun or an adjective, must have a child word in the nsubj or nsubjpass relation.

[5]The target word cannot be repeated in the rest of the sentence.

| **Method:** | Co-occur |
| **Related word:** | *xiangbi* 相比 'compare' (Highest PMI with target word) |

與其他生物 [相比 (*xiangbi*)]，人類的生產過程顯得 (*xiande*) 複雜許多。
When [compared] with other organisms, the human reproductive process appears a lot more complex.

| **Method:** | Similar |
| **Related word:** | *gengwei* 更為 'even more' (Highest similarity score with target word) |

在政治和宗教的問題上，牛津比劍橋顯得 (*xiande*)[更為 (*gengwei*)] 保守。
On political and religious issues, Oxford appears [even more] conservative than Cambridge.

Table 1: Carrier sentences selected for the target word *xiande* 'appear, seem, look' by the Co-occur method and Similar method.

Method	Sentence Score		Word Score	
	Avg	Good	Avg	Good
Baseline	2.15	50%	2.60	77%
+Similar	2.51	71%	2.67	80%
+Co-occur	**2.68**	**79%**	**2.70**	**82%**
Human	**2.70**	**81%**	**2.91**	**94%**

Table 2: Percentage of sentences rated "Good" (score 3 out of 3) and scores of carrier sentences generated by the various methods, averaged between the two judges

that they are roughly equally spaced in the list of 20,000 most frequent words in the Wiki Set. For each of these 100 words, we retrieve candidate sentences from the Wiki Set that satisfy the constraints imposed by the **Baseline** features. From this pool of candidates, we used three methods to select a carrier sentence. The Baseline method randomly selects a sentence from the pool. The +Similar method selects the candidate that optimizes the **Lexical Similarity** feature. The +Co-occur method selects the candidate that optimizes the **Word co-occurrence** feature. Finally, the Human method uses the carrier sentence from the Textbook Set.

We asked two human judges, both native Chinese speakers, to evaluate the four carrier sentences for each of the 100 target words. They assigned two scores to each sentence: the *Sentence Score* (3="Good", 2="Fair", 1="Unacceptable") assesses the extent to which the sentence is grammatical, fluent and fit for pedagogical purpose; the *Word Score*, on the same 3-point scale, indicates how well the sentence succeeds in illustrating a typical usage of the target word. The kappa for these two scores are 0.342 and 0.227, respectively; both are considered a "fair" level of agreement (Landis and Koch, 1977).

5 Experimental results

As shown in Table 2, human-authored carrier sentences attracted the highest scores, and have the highest percentage rated "Good" (81.0% and 93.5% for the sentence and word scores). In terms of the Sentence Score, both the Co-occur method and Similar method[6] outperformed the baseline. For the Co-occur method, 79.0% of the sentences were rated "Good". In most cases, the presence of a word of frequent co-occurrence seemed to be a reliable indicator of a high-quality sentence. The Word Score tends to be high across all methods; the baseline features already led to 77.0% of the selected sentences rated "Good". Both the Co-occur and Similar methods only slightly outperformed the baseline[7], suggesting a relatively high quality of word usage in general in Chinese Wikipedia articles.

6 Conclusions

We have presented a study on automatic selection of carrier sentences for fill-in-the-blank items for Chinese as a foreign language. Our evaluation results show that word co-occurrence and lexical similarity measures can improve the quality of the carrier sentences, over a baseline that considers only sentence complexity, vocabulary difficulty, sentence completeness, and target word position.

Acknowledgments

This work is funded by the Language Fund under Research and Development Projects 2015-2016 of the Standing Committee on Language Education and Research (SCOLAR), Hong Kong SAR.

---

[6]$p < 0.001$ by McNemar's test for both methods
[7]Not statistically significant, at $p = 0.34$ and $p = 0.54$ by McNemar's test

References

Vít Baisa and Vít Suchomel. 2014. SkELL: Web Interface for English Language Learning. In *Proc. Recent Advances in Slavonic Natural Language Processing*.

Chia-Yin Chen, Hsien-Chin Liou, and Jason S. Chang. 2006. FAST: An Automatic Generation System for Grammar Tests. In *Proc. COLING/ACL Interactive Presentation Sessions*.

Yu-Ta Chen, Yaw-Huei Chen, and Yu-Chih Cheng. 2013. Assessing chinese readability using term frequency and lexical chain. *Computational Linguistics and Chinese Language Processing* 18(2):1–18.

Kevyn Collins-Thompson. 2008. Computational assessment of text readability: A survey of current and future research. *International Journal of Applied Linguistics* 165(2):97–135.

Jörg Didakowski, Lothar Lemnitzer, and Alexander Geyken. 2012. Automatic Example Sentence Extraction for a Contemporary German Dictionary. In *Proc. EURALEX*.

T. M. Haladyna, S. M. Downing, and M. C. Rodriguez. 2002. A Review of Multiple-Choice Item-Writing Guidelines for Classroom Assessment. *Applied Measurement in Education* 15(3):309–333.

Rohit J. Kate, Xiaoqiang Luo, Siddharth Patwardhan, Martin Franz, Radu Florian, Raymond J. Mooney, Salim Roukos, and Chris Welty. 2010. Learning to Predict Readability using Diverse Linguistic Features. In *Proc. 23rd International Conference on Computational Linguistics (COLING)*. pages 546–554.

Adam Kilgarriff, Mils Husák, Katy McAdam, Michael Rundell, and Pavel Rychlý. 2008. GDEX: Automatically Finding Good Dictionary Examples in a Corpus. In *Proc. EURALEX*.

Susanne Knoop and Sabrina Wilske. 2013. WordGap: Automatic Generation of Gap-Filling Vocabulary Exercises for Mobile Learning. In *Proc. Second Workshop on NLP for Computer-assisted Language Learning, NODALIDA*.

J. Richard Landis and Gary G. Koch. 1977. The Measurement of Observer Agreement for Categorical Data. *Biometrics* 33:159–174.

Roger Levy and Christopher D. Manning. 2003. Is it harder to parse Chinese, or the Chinese Treebank? In *Proc. ACL*.

Chao-Lin Liu, Chun-Hung Wang, Zhao-Ming Gao, and Shang-Ming Huang. 2005. Applications of Lexical Information for Algorithmically Composing Multiple-Choice Cloze Items. In *Proc. 2nd Workshop on Building Educational Applications Using NLP*. pages 1–8.

Jennifer Lichia Liu. 2004. *Connections I: a Cognitive Approach to Intermediate Chinese*. Indiana University Press, Bloomington, IN.

Jennifer Lichia Liu. 2010. *Encounters I/II: a Cognitive Approach to Advanced Chinese*. Indiana University Press, Bloomington, IN.

Detmar Meurers, Ramon Ziai, Luiz Amaral, Adriane Boyd, Aleksandar Dimitrov, Vanessa Metcalf, and Niels Ott. 2010. Enhancing Authentic Web Pages for Language Learners. In *Proc. Fifth Workshop on Innovative Use of Nlp for Building Educational Applications*.

Tomas Mikolov, Kai Chen, Greg Corrado, and Jeffrey Dean. 2013. Efficient estimation of word representations in vector space. In *Proc. ICLR*.

Ildikó Pilán, Elena Volodina, and Richard Johansson. 2013. Automatic Selection of Suitable Sentences for Language Learning Exercises. In *Proc. EURO-CALL*.

Ildikó Pilán, Elena Volodina, and Richard Johansson. 2014. Rule-based and Machine Learning Approaches for Second Language Sentence-level Readability. In *Proc. 9th Workshop on Innovative Use of NLP for Building Educational Applications*.

Juan Pino and Maxine Eskenazi. 2009. Semi-automatic Generation of Cloze Question Distractors: Effect of Students' L1. In *Proc. SLaTE*.

Emily Pitler and Ani Nenkova. 2008. Revisiting readability: a unified framework for predicting text quality. In *Proc. EMNLP*.

Keisuke Sakaguchi, Yuki Arase, and Mamoru Komachi. 2013. Discriminative Approach to Fill-in-the-Blank Quiz Generation for Language Learners. In *Proc. ACL*.

Sarah E. Schwarm and Mari Ostendorf. 2005. Reading level assessment using support vector machines and statistical language models. In *Proc. ACL*.

Simon Smith, P. V. S. Avinesh, and Adam Kilgarriff. 2010. Gap-fill Tests for Language Learners: Corpus-Driven Item Generation. In *Proc. 8th International Conference on Natural Language Processing (ICON)*.

Simon Smith, Adam Kilgarriff, W-L Gong, S. Sommers, and G-Z Wu. 2009. Automatic Cloze Generation for English Proficiency Testing. In *Proc. LTTC Conference*.

Eiichiro Sumita, Fumiaki Sugaya, and Seiichi Yamamoto. 2005. Measuring Non-native Speakers' Proficiency of English by Using a Test with Automatically-Generated Fill-in-the-Blank Questions. In *Proc. 2nd Workshop on Building Educational Applications using NLP*.

Yao-Ting Sung, Ju-Ling Chen, Ji-Her Cha, Hou-Chiang Tseng, Tao-Hsing Chang, and Kuo-En Chang. 2015. Constructing and validating readability models: the method of integrating multilevel linguistic features with machine learning. *Behavior Research Methods* 47:340–354.

Elena Volodina, Richard Johansson, and Sofie Johansson Kokkinakis. 2012. Semi-automatic Selection of Best Corpus Examples for Swedish: Initial Algorithm Evaluation. In *Proc. Workshop on NLP in Computer-Assisted Language Learning*.

Youmin Wang. 2007. 實用商務漢語課本（漢韓版）準高級篇／高級篇. Commercial Press, Beijing.

Wei Xu. 2012. A Research on Blanked Cloze Exercises in Intermediate TCSL Comprehensive Textbooks Taking Four Textbooks as Examples [in Chinese]. In 第五届北京地区对外汉语教学研究生论坛 *(Proc. 5th Forum of CFL Graduate Students)*. School of Chinese as a Second Language, Peking University, Beijing, China.

Torsten Zesch and Oren Melamud. 2014. Automatic Generation of Challenging Distractors Using Context-Sensitive Inference Rules. In *Proc. Workshop on Innovative Use of NLP for Building Educational Applications (BEA)*.

Hindi Shabdamitra:
A Wordnet based E-Learning Tool for Language Learning and Teaching

Hanumant Redkar, Sandhya Singh, Meenakshi Somasundaram,
Dhara Gorasia, Malhar Kulkarni and Pushpak Bhattacharyya

Center for Indian Language Technology,
Department of Computer Science and Engineering,
Indian Institute of Technology Bombay, Mumbai, India.
{hanumantredkar, sandhya.singh, meenakshi.somasundaram}@gmail.com,
{dharagorasiya, malharku and pushpakbh}@gmail.com

Abstract

In today's technology driven digital era, education domain is undergoing a transformation from traditional approaches to more learner controlled and flexible methods of learning. This transformation has opened the new avenues for interdisciplinary research in the field of educational technology and natural language processing in developing quality digital aids for learning and teaching. The tool presented here - *Hindi Shabhadamitra*, developed using Hindi Wordnet for Hindi language learning, is one such e-learning tool. It has been developed as a teaching and learning aid suitable for formal school based curriculum and informal setup for self learning users. Besides vocabulary, it also provides word based grammar along with images and pronunciation for better learning and retention. This aid demonstrates that how a rich lexical resource like wordnet can be systematically remodeled for practical usage in the educational domain.

1 Introduction

With technology expanding into every domain of society, its impact is visible in the education domain as well. And with improving infrastructure and better technologies the digitization in education is here to stay. Another important catalyst in this area is the receptiveness of the entities involved *viz.* students and teachers.

The technology has provided an edge by reducing the cost of delivering the education to volume of students. Due to its multi-sensory impact, the researchers have proved that, e-learning enhances the students' outcome (Shams and Seitz, 2008; Sankey et al., 2010). With all these benefits, the need for quality digital aids for learning becomes imminent.

As the trend of global citizen is becoming more prevalent, the knowledge of multiple language becomes preferable. For any language learning activity, vocabulary learning is considered central (Alqahtani et al., 2015). Besides this, the other directions of language learning include grammar learning, conversational usage, colloquial usage, literary usage, *etc.* Digital language learning aids are a big support in this direction.

Understanding a word involves - committing to memory its form, capturing its relationship with other words and finally knowing how and where to use it. Vocabulary learning methods (Nation and Newton, 1997; Dunlosky et al., 2013; Oxford, 2016) vary from –

- Directly learning the language without any intervention of the mother tongue.

- Translating the words from target language to mother tongue of the learner in order to convey the meaning.

- Highlighting the new words in a given text and finding out its meaning with the help of a glossary or synonyms.

Keeping vocabulary and grammar learning as pivotal to language learning, an e-learning tool, *Hindi Shabdamitra*, has been developed.

This paper presents a digital Hindi language teaching and learning aid, *Hindi Shabdamitra*, which is mainly a vocabulary and word specific grammar learning aid for formal and informal setups of language learning. It uses Hindi Wordnet[1] as a resource for vocabulary teaching.

The rest of the paper is organized as follows: section 2 gives information about the related work, section 3 introduces the *Hindi Shabdamitra*, section 4 provides the user field response, which is followed by conclusion and future work.

---

[1] http://www.cfilt.iitb.ac.in/wordnet/ webhwn/wn.php

23

Proceedings of the 4th Workshop on Natural Language Processing Techniques for Educational Applications, pages 23–28,
Taipei, Taiwan, December 1, 2017 ©2017 AFNLP

2   Related Work

The literature about vocabulary learning strategies, language learning psychology and digital educational applications shows that multi-modal learning always result in better retention (Dale, 1969). Vocabulary is cited as the one of the primary reasons for learner's ability and confidence to communicate. Various mechanical strategies like repetition, context, usage and visual correlation have been tested by language experts for enhancing the vocabulary (Atasheneh and Naeimi, 2015; Butler et al., 2010). When the information enters the system through various senses, the brain tries to overcome the limited processing abilities of each individual senses, which results in better information processing (Clark and Paivio, 1991). The multi-modal learning environments have been studied in different settings (Mayer and Moreno, 2003; Moreno and Mayer, 2007; Shams and Seitz, 2008; Sankey et al., 2010) which shows its positive impact on learners. To enhance the willingness of the learner for self-directed technology (Lai et al., 2016), Mobile Assisted Language Learning (MALL) (Yang, 2013) and gamification is seen as an effective pedagogical strategy. These strategies help to engage and motivate the learner to learn in a relaxed environment (Werbach and Hunter, 2012; Figueroa Flores, 2015).

Semantic relations of words have shown to help in better understanding of new vocabulary (Lin, 1997). The wordnet[2], a rich lexical resource based on semantic relations, have been explored for vocabulary learning and other related language learning applications (Hu et al., 1998; Sun et al., 2011; Brumbaugh, 2015; Hiray, 2015).

3   *Hindi Shabdamitra*: An E-Learning Teaching Aid

3.1   Background

Hindi written in Devanagari script is the official language of the Republic of India. It is one of the widely spoken languages in India. For learning Hindi, a lot of digital content is available online in the form of games, stories, poems and theme based conversation, along with basic knowledge of grammar and vocabulary. The content delivered to learners *via* subscribed Youtube videos, subscribed web interfaces, social media websites, live skype lectures, purchasable DVDs, *etc*. Some of

the applications for language learning which offer Hindi learning are - Duolingo[3], Hindipod[4], Rocket Language[5], Italki[6], *etc*. Some applications meant specifically for children are dinolingo[7], akhlesh[8], galligallisimsim[9], *etc*. Other online resources for Hindi language are bilingual dictionaries which provide only the meanings of the words, such as Shabdkosh[10], Collins dictionary[11], *etc*. The commonality among all the above resources is their inability of customization for formal school setups. They are more focused for individual learning.

As per renowned teaching methodology and vocabulary acquisition researcher, Prof. Paul Nation, vocabulary teaching should be done in a structured way (Nation and Newton, 1997; Carter, 1987; Lin, 1997). The aim should be to improve the passive knowledge and make the learner able to use the words in their day-to-day communication.

A study of current digital resources used by various educational institution was also done as part of the background study. The outcome showed a big gap of quality resources which can cover all aspects of language learning like grammar, concepts, usage and pronunciations in an effective manner.

This motivation led to the development of a digital aid that would fill this gap for Hindi language learning. Through the e-learning tool presented here *Hindi Shabdamitra*, an attempt has been made to teach and learn Hindi language in both formal and informal settings, along with learning of the word based grammatical features. Further, this tool facilitates learning with the help of illustrations and pronunciation for multi-sensory impact.

3.2   Hindi Shabdamitra

Hindi Shabdamitra (हिंदी शब्दमित्र)[12] is a digital aid designed for assisting in learning and teaching of Hindi language. It is developed in correlation with school curriculum, which is considered here as a formal setup of learning. Along with schools, it can also be used by individuals or organizations not following any specific curriculum *viz*. NGOs, for-

---

[2]https://wordnet.princeton.edu/

[3]https://www.duolingo.com/
[4]https://www.hindipod101.com/
[5]https://www.rocketlanguages.com
[6]https://www.italki.com
[7]https://dinolingo.com
[8]http://www.akhlesh.com/
[9]http://www.galligallisimsim.com/
[10]www.shabdkosh.com/
[11]https://www.collinsdictionary.com
[12]http://www.cfilt.iitb.ac.in/
hindishabdamitra/

Figure 1: Class wise and Level wise search interface selection

eign Universities teaching Hindi, self learners, *etc.*, which is considered as a non formal setup of learning. It uses Hindi Wordnet as a base resource that has been remodeled for this aid by incorporating the multi-modal features. Further, The concepts are grammatically enriched and simplified depending upon the understanding level of the learner.

As small children learn easily and effortlessly if a picture is provided rather than a text content. Hence, for the initial phase, concepts are pictorially depicted by providing illustrations for level 1 and 2, so that a given concept can be easily captured by these kids. The illustrations are digitally drawn by the in-house illustrators keeping the sense of a concept in mind. Most of the illustrations are simple and shows positivity and happiness, and conveys the right information.

Also, search-words are provided with the audio pronunciation. These words are recorded by native speakers of the language in the standard Hindi format.

A team of lexicographers, illustrators and native language speakers have contributed to build this multi-modal resource which has formed the base of *Hindi Shabdamitra*. The tool has an online web-based and app-based interface for wider reachability. Also, this tool can be made available offline for anytime anywhere learning. The interface allows the search navigation in two ways – level wise (हिंदी ज्ञान स्तर के अनुसार, *hiMdii GYaana stara ke anusaara*) and class wise (कक्षा के अनुसार, *kaxaa ke anusaara*). This can be seen in figure 1.

The unique features of this E-learning tool are –

- It is meant for Hindi language learning, in sync with school curriculum

- It allows vocabulary and word related grammatical feature learning

- It can be used for formal *i.e.*, school curriculum based setup and informal *i.e.*, individual based setup of learning and teaching

- It has a multifaceted design having pictures and audio pronunciation

- It provides learning through layered interface for wider audience

- It allows student and teacher participation and engagement

- It has a learner friendly interface for ease of learning

- It is accessible on mobiles, smart devices, computers, *etc.*

- It is available in online and off-line mode.

This tool can assist the teachers in better classroom management and make learning Hindi an interesting activity. Also, this tool can assist self learners using the layered approach.

3.3 Resource used: Hindi Wordnet

Hindi Wordnet, a digital language resource, is an online lexical repository having synonymy set called as synset. Synset contains a gloss (definition) and an example sentence. Wordnet is linked by semantic relations like hypernymy (is-a), meronymy (part-of), troponymy (manner-of), *etc.* and by lexical relations like antonymy, gradation, *etc.* (Bhattacharyya, 2010). It was originally developed for the research in the area of Natural Language Processing. Hindi wordnet, being a rich lexical resource, which is a dictionary cum thesaurus, have been used as a resource for the development of this digital aid. In particular, the tool uses Hindi wordnet's gloss, examples, synonyms, ontological information, lexico-semantic relations. Some of the above information is modified as per the level of the learner.

3.4 A Layered Interface

Hindi Shabdamitra has been designed for a wider range of target audience. Keeping in sight the level of the learners, the interface has a layered architecture. It has the following five layers:

Figure 2: Class wise search in *Hindi Shabdamitra*

- Level 1 (for classes 1 and 2)

- Level 2 (for classes 3, 4 and 5)

- Level 3 (for classes 6, 7, 8, 9 and 10)

- Level 4 (for classes 11 and 12)

- Level 5 (for classes above 12, researchers, language learners, *etc.*)

The same search-word can be studied by the learners of all 5 levels. At each level incremental information is displayed. The depth of content displayed in terms of synonyms, grammatical information, ontological information will vary from level to level.

3.4.1 Class-wise Search Selection

The tool has been devised keeping in mind the different school curriculum based on the affiliations to various governing bodies responsible for standardization of school education, *i.e.*, CBSE[13], ICSE[14], state boards, *etc.* In class-wise search, a 'board' is selected followed by 'class number' and 'lesson number'. This selection allows the teacher to choose the words from the syllabus which she/he is going to teach in class to students. The major advantage here is that the tool covers all the vocabulary in a given class as these words were manually collected from the school curriculum. This will assist teacher in teaching all possible words available in a given lesson. At the same time, the word related grammatical features like gender, countability, *etc.* and lexico-semantic relations like antonyms, synonyms, *etc.* can be taught to students. Figure 2 shows an instance of class wise search explaining the concept of a word 'माँ' (*maa* ,

a mother). In this example only परिभाषा (*paribhaaShaa*, a gloss or concept definition), वाक्य में प्रयोग (*vaakya meM prayoga*, usage in an example), बहुवचन (*bahuvachana*, plural) and समानार्थी शब्द (*samaanaarthii shabda*, synonyms) has been selectively displayed. Here, for class 1 to class 5 the gloss and example sentence from original Hindi Wordnet is further simplified by providing the simple words in the definition so that the students at these levels can easily pick-up and learn concept comfortably. At the higher classes the more information like lexico-semantic relations like hypernymy, holonymy, *etc.* along with grammatical features like transitivity, kind of noun or verb, *etc.*, is provided.

3.4.2 Level-wise Search Selection

Level wise search interface is designed for the informal non-curriculum based scenario where any person can learn a given word and understand it at his/her own pace. In this interface, the search is not restricted to the vocabulary of a given class and lesson. Here the learner has two options to follow. One, where the learner is not sure of his/her expertise of knowledge. In such case, the information can be accessed in small portions so that the learner is able to grasp it better. Once comfortable with the low level content, the learner can opt for more detailed information about the search-word. The other flow, where the learner is aware and can choose the level based on his/her knowledge.

Level 1 is for beginners, level 2 is for intermediate learners, level 3 for proficient, level 4 for advanced and level 5 for experts. The amount of information displayed is varied based on the level selected. In each level the information is rendered based on its part-of-speech category and grammatical properties.

Figure 3 shows the level wise search for level 2. In this figure, the information rendered in Hindi is परिभाषा (*paribhaaShaa*, a gloss or concept definition), वाक्य में प्रयोग (*vaakya meM prayoga*, usage in an example), बहुवचन (*bahuvachana*, plural), समानार्थी शब्द (*samaanaarthii shabda*, synonyms), लिंग (*liMga*, gender), संज्ञा के प्रकार (*saMGYaa ke prakaara*, kind of noun) and गणनीयता (*gaNaniiyataa*, countability). Like Class-wise, there can be more information at each levels depending upon the part-of-speech category and the grammatical features of a search-word.

Since, this is an era of smart devices such as mobiles, tablets, *etc.*, the android based mobile app

---

[13]http://cbse.nic.in/newsite/index.html
[14]http://www.cisce.org/

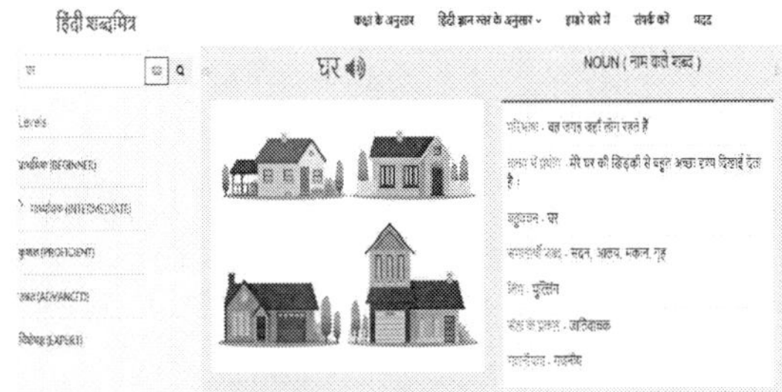

Figure 3: Level wise search in *Hindi Shabdamitra* for *Intermediate learner* (Level 2)

have been developed. Figure 4 shows the developed mobile interface for *Hindi Shabdamitra*.

4   Field Response

As part of testing the tool, the field trial of the *Hindi Shabdamitra*'s web and app interface was done at 3 local schools with around 400 students and 10 teachers participating in the exercise. The feedback was sought for the content, ease of handling the application, classroom impact and overall experience by teachers and students. Our observation and feedback from the teachers clearly indicate that it helped teachers in explaining concepts clearly with the help of illustrations and simplified concepts. Audio clips helped in understanding the pronunciation of a given word. The aid assisted the teacher in better classroom management, reduced effort of reiterating the concepts for better retention and having the standardized pronunciation by the native Hindi speaker. The application has been

Figure 4: Mobile App for *Hindi Shabdamitra*

improved based on the feedback received by students and teachers.

5   Conclusion and Future Work

With technological advancement, education domain is shifting from a traditional knowledge-transfer model to a collaborative, multi-sensory, self-paced, engaging model with the flexibility of anywhere anytime learning. Based on Hindi Wordnet, *Hindi Shabdamitra* is one such comprehensive e-learning tool which helps in learning Hindi language, pronunciation, grammar and understanding the concepts through illustrations, definition and examples. It caters to a wide range of audience and is available in both web based and app based formats for flexibility of usage. It is well received by the learners in the initial phase of launch. This aid shows how a semantically rich lexical resource like Wordnet, originally developed for research purpose, can be modeled for practical usage in education domain.

In future, the authors intend to include interactive assessment module for evaluations and other game based assessment modules for fun learning. It can be extended for learning other Indian languages. Further, the illustrations, audio, grammatical features, simplified gloss, *etc.* of *Hindi Shabdamitra* can act as an enriched resource.

Acknowledgements

The authors would like to thank and acknowledge the support and help by the members of Center for Indian Language Technology (CFILT)[15] and *Hindi Shabdamitra* team. The funding agency, Tata Center for Technology and Design (TCTD)[16] has been instrumental and supportive throughout the development of *Hindi Shabdamitra*.

References

Mofareh Alqahtani et al. 2015. The importance of vocabulary in language learning and how to be taught. *International Journal of Teaching and Education* 3(3):21–34.

Nasser Atasheneh and Maki Naeimi. 2015. Vocabulary learning through using mechanical techniques vocabulary learning strategy. *Theory and Practice in Language Studies* 5(3):541.

---

[15]`http://www.cfilt.iitb.ac.in`
[16]`http://www.tatacentre.iitb.ac.in/digital_aid.php`

Pushpak Bhattacharyya. 2010. Indowordnet. In *The WordNet in Indian Languages*, Springer, pages 1–18.

Heidi Brumbaugh. 2015. *Self-assigned ranking of L2 vocabulary: using the Bricklayer computer game to assess depth of word knowledge*. Ph.D. thesis, Arts & Social Sciences:.

Shari Butler, Kelsi Urrutia, Anneta Buenger, Nina Gonzalez, M Hunt, and Corinne Eisenhart. 2010. A review of the current research on vocabulary instruction. *National Reading Technical Assistance Center, RMC Research Corporation* 1.

Ronald Carter. 1987. Vocabulary and second/foreign language teaching. *Language Teaching* 20(01):3–16.

James M Clark and Allan Paivio. 1991. Dual coding theory and education. *Educational psychology review* 3(3):149–210.

Edgar Dale. 1969. Audiovisual methods in teaching .

John Dunlosky, Katherine A Rawson, Elizabeth J Marsh, Mitchell J Nathan, and Daniel T Willingham. 2013. Improving students' learning with effective learning techniques: Promising directions from cognitive and educational psychology. *Psychological Science in the Public Interest* 14(1):4–58.

Jorge Francisco Figueroa Flores. 2015. Using gamification to enhance second language learning. *Digital Education Review* 27:32–54.

Amit C. Hiray. 2015. *Teaching and Learning of EAP Vocabulary: A Web-based Integrative Approach at the Tertiary Level in India*. Ph.D. thesis, Dept. of HSS, IIT Bombay.

X Hu, AC Graesser, Tutoring Research Group, et al. 1998. Using wordnet and latent semantic analysis to evaluate the conversational contributions of learners in the tutorial dialog. In *Proceedings of the international conference on computers in education*. volume 2, pages 337–341.

Chun Lai, Mark Shum, and Yan Tian. 2016. Enhancing learners' self-directed use of technology for language learning: the effectiveness of an online training platform. *Computer Assisted Language Learning* 29(1):40–60.

Chih-Cheng Lin. 1997. Semantic network for vocabulary teaching.   :   (42):43–54.

Richard E Mayer and Roxana Moreno. 2003. Nine ways to reduce cognitive load in multimedia learning. *Educational psychologist* 38(1):43–52.

Roxana Moreno and Richard Mayer. 2007. Interactive multimodal learning environments. *Educational psychology review* 19(3):309–326.

Paul Nation and Jonathan Newton. 1997. Teaching vocabulary. *Second language vocabulary acquisition* pages 238–254.

Rebecca L Oxford. 2016. *Teaching and researching language learning strategies: Self-regulation in context*. Taylor & Francis.

Michael Sankey, Dawn Birch, and Michael Gardiner. 2010. Engaging students through multimodal learning environments: The journey continues. In *Proceedings ASCILITE 2010: 27th Annual Conference of the Australasian Society for Computers in Learning in Tertiary Education: Curriculum, Technology and Transformation for an Unknown Future*. University of Queensland, pages 852–863.

Ladan Shams and Aaron R Seitz. 2008. Benefits of multisensory learning. *Trends in cognitive sciences* 12(11):411–417.

Koun-Tem Sun, Huang Yueh-Min, and Liu Ming-Chi. 2011. A wordnet-based near-synonyms and similar-looking word learning system. *Journal of Educational Technology & Society* 14(1):121.

Kevin Werbach and Dan Hunter. 2012. *For the win: How game thinking can revolutionize your business*. Wharton Digital Press.

Jaeseok Yang. 2013. Mobile assisted language learning: review of the recent applications of emerging mobile technologies. *English Language Teaching* 6(7):19–25.

NLPTEA 2017 Shared Task – Chinese Spelling Check

Gabriel Pui Cheong Fung[*], Maxime Debosschere[*], Dingmin Wang[*§],
Bo Li[*], Jia Zhu[‡], and Kam-Fai Wong[*]

[*] Department of Sys. Eng. & Eng. Mgt., The Chinese University of Hong Kong, China
{pcfung, dmaxime, boli, kfwong}@se.cuhk.edu.hk

[‡] Department of Computer Science, South China Normal University, China
jzhu@m.scnu.edu.cn

[§] Department of Computer Science, Tsinghua University, China
wangdm15@mails.tsinghua.edu.cn

Abstract

This paper provides an overview along with our findings of the Chinese Spelling Check shared task at NLPTEA 2017. The goal of this task is to develop a computer-assisted system to automatically diagnose typing errors in traditional Chinese sentences written by students. We defined six types of errors which belong to two categories. Given a sentence, the system should detect where the errors are, and for each detected error determine its type and provide correction suggestions. We designed, constructed, and released a benchmark dataset for this task.

1 Introduction

Automatic spelling checking is the task of using machines to automatically detect writing errors (Mays et al., 1991). Most popular word processors have this capability for alphabet-based languages, such as English, French and German, but not for character-based languages, such as Chinese.

In this shared task, we focus on spelling checking Chinese, which is very different than checking alphabetic languages due to several distinct properties of the Chinese language:

1. There is a vast variety of characters. There exist more than 100,000 Chinese characters, around 3,500 of which constitute the common characters of modern Chinese. Many characters have similar shapes and/or similar pronunciations.

2. There are no delimiters between words.

3. Each character has a meaning. Furthermore, the length of words is usually very short, ranging between one and four characters.

4. Depending on their positions in a sentence, identical characters or words can sometimes belong to different kinds of part of speech (verb, noun, etc.).

5. There exist many colloquial words and phrases that do not occur in written Chinese. This property becomes especially obvious in Cantonese, which is a dialect of Chinese. There is a significant number of words, phrases, and sentence structures that are valid in daily conversation, yet are considered invalid when written down.

We observed that publicly available benchmark data for Chinese spelling checking is limited. To make matters worse, no benchmark dataset targets the last of the aforementioned properties. This motivated us to develop a new benchmark dataset which takes colloquialism into account, and which is publicly available in order to promote future research of Chinese spelling checking in this area.

In general, a good spelling checker is able to detect errors and provide correction suggestions for each detected error. Since every character in Chinese has a meaning (i.e., every character can always be regarded as a word, which is very different from alphabetic-based languages), spelling checks must be done within a context, such as a sentence or a long phrase with a certain meaning, rather than within very few words (Mays et al., 1991). Accordingly, we collected a number of students' writings to serve as the benchmark data for this shared task.

Proceedings of the 4th Workshop on Natural Language Processing Techniques for Educational Applications, pages 29–34,
Taipei, Taiwan, December 1, 2017 ©2017 AFNLP

For the evaluation, it should be noted that we do not have any widely recognised or standard evaluation schemas specifically designed for evaluating the performance of Chinese spelling checkers. Nonetheless, different evaluation schemas have been proposed for different purposes (Duan et al., 2012; Tseng et al., 2015; Wu et al., 2013; Yu et al., 2008, 2014; Zhao and Liu, 2010). Since we could not find any existing evaluation schema that fulfils all our evaluation criteria, we proposed a new evaluation schema in this task. We understand that this proposed evaluation schema may not be perfect, however it does capture most essential elements for considering whether a spelling checker is effective.

The rest of this paper is organised as follows: Section 2 describes the benchmark dataset, Section 3 presents the tasks, Section 4 outlines the evaluation schema, and Section 5 reports the findings and concludes this paper.

2 Benchmark Dataset

The Hong Kong Applied Science and Technology Research Institute (ASTRI), founded by the Government of the Hong Kong Special Administrative Region in 2000, first collected more than 5,000 writings by Hong Kong primary students. We then invited researchers from the Department of Chinese Language and Literature at The Chinese University of Hong Kong to help mark and annotate these writings. Next, we extracted sentences with at least one error, and from this subset we manually filtered all sentences which are semantically meaningful, have a reasonable length, and are easy to understand without additional context. A total of 6,890 sentences met these criteria. Each sentence contains 50 to 150 characters, including punctuation marks. The average number of errors in a sentence is 2.7, and the maximum is 5. Finally, we defined the following six types of errors:

1. Typo – Similar shape. E.g., in the word 辨論, 辨 is a typo and should be written as 辯. 辨 and 辯 have similar shapes.

2. Typo – Similar pronunciation. E.g., in the word 今荀, 今 is a typo and should be replaced by 甘. 今 and 甘 have similar pronunciations in Cantonese.

3. Typo – Mixing simplified and traditional Chinese. E.g., for the word 词語, 词 is simplified Chinese and should be replaced by its traditional counterpart 詞.

4. Colloquialism – Incorrect character. E.g., for the sentence "佢比你高" the character 佢 is colloquial and should be changed into formal writing: either 他 or 她.

5. Colloquialism – Incorrect word or phrase. All characters are proper formal Chinese, but when combined they form a colloquial word. E.g., in the sentence "昨天撞返一個很久沒有見面的小學同學" the word 撞返 is colloquial even though the characters 撞 and 返 are both formal written Chinese. Here, 撞返 should be replaced by 碰見.

6. Colloquialism – Incorrect usage. All characters are properly written without any colloquial characters or words or phrases, but the ordering of some characters or words is incorrect, resulting in colloquial language. E.g., in the sentence "我走先了" the word 走先 is colloquial and should be written as 先走.

We classify the first three types of errors as "typos" and the last three types of errors as "colloquialisms". Since all the writings in our dataset came from Hong Kong students, all colloquialisms in our dataset are Cantonese. Note that it is possible to have any mixture of the above cases, even if just colloquialisms. For example, consider the sentence "大家討論緊這件事". In this context, the character 緊 is a colloquial word and means 正在 (error type 4 in the aforementioned classification). Yet, simply replacing 緊 by 正在 is still wrong since it then triggers error type 5. Instead, the correction should be "大家正在討論這件事".

Since our benchmark dataset also required positive examples, we manually added 3,110 entirely correct sentences from our collection of writings, reaching a round total of 10,000 sentences. Next, we randomly selected 1,000 sentences from our dataset as training data, and another 1,000 sentences as testing data. To the best of our knowledge, there is no publicly available benchmark dataset that takes into account all six types of errors outlined above. We are the first to release such dataset, and it can be obtained from the project website.[1]

---

[1] https://www.labviso.com/nlptea2017/download/

3 Tasks: Detection and Correction

The objective of this shared task is to develop
a computer-assisted system that automatically di-
agnoses typing errors in traditional Chinese sentences written by native Hong Kong primary students.

3.1 Overview

As mentioned in Section 2, there are two categories of errors: typos and colloquialisms. A sentence may be free of errors, have one error, or have
multiple errors. Here are some additional examples:

- No error:
  我很喜歡吃媽媽做的瓜炒蛋飯。

- Typo only:
  我很喜歡吃媽媽做的<u>梁</u>瓜炒蛋飯。

- Colloquialism only:
  我很<u>鍾意</u>吃媽媽做的瓜炒蛋飯。

- Typo and colloquialism:
  我很<u>鍾意</u>吃媽媽做的<u>梁</u>瓜炒蛋飯。

- Multiple typos and multiple colloquialisms:
  我很<u>鍾意食</u>媽媽做的<u>梁</u>瓜炒<u>旦</u>飯。

As this is the first time we have colloquialisms
in benchmark data, we provide a Cantonese-
Chinese mapping dictionary in this shared task.
This dictionary is in JSON format and contains all
mappings between Cantonese and formal written
Chinese. All Cantonese language that appears in
the training and testing datasets is guaranteed to be
included in this file. Note that a Cantonese phrase
may have more than one possible mapping (depending on the context of the sentence) and different combinations of words in a phrase may yield
entirely different results. For example:

```
{"cantonese":"唔", "chinese":["不"]},
{"cantonese":"唔使", "chinese":["不用"]},
{"cantonese":"唔該", "chinese":["請","謝
    謝"]},
{"cantonese":"邊度", "chinese":["哪裏"]},
{"cantonese":"邊處", "chinese":["哪裏"]}
```

We provide the training data, testing data, and
their corresponding gold standards. Everything is
in JSON format. For example, given the following
sentences:

```
{
  "id":"ASTRI01",
  "sentence":"我很喜歡吃媽媽做的涼瓜炒蛋飯。"
},
{
  "id":"ASTRI02",
  "sentence":"我很喜歡吃媽媽做的梁瓜炒蛋飯。"
},
{
  "id":"ASTRI03",
  "sentence":"我很鍾意吃媽媽做的涼瓜炒蛋飯。"
},
{
  "id":"ASTRI04",
  "sentence":"我很鍾意食媽媽做的梁瓜炒旦飯。"
}
```

the corresponding gold standard is:

```
{
  "id":"ASTRI01",
  "typo":null,
  "cantonese":null
},
{
  "id":"ASTRI02",
  "typo":[
    {
      "position":10,
      "correction":["涼"]
    }],
  "cantonese":null,
  "reorder":null
},
{
  "id":"ASTRI03",
  "typo":null,
  "cantonese":[
    {
      "position":3,
      "length":2,
      "correction":["喜歡"]
    }],
  "reorder":null
},
{
  "id":"ASTRI04",
  "typo":[
    {
      "position":10,
      "correction":["涼"]
    },
    {
      "position":13,
      "correction":["蛋"]
    }],
  "cantonese":[
    {
      "position":3,
      "length":2,
      "correction":["喜歡"]
    },
    {
```

```
      "position":5,
      "length":1,
      "correction":["吃"]
    }],
    "reorder":null
}
```

The structure and meaning of the above examples should be self-explanatory. Note that according to Section 2, there are multiple types of colloquialism. This is the reason why the "reorder" field is necessary for colloquialism detection in a sentence. To illustrate this necessity, observe that when given the following sentences:

```
{
  "id":"ASTRI05",
  "sentence":"我走先然後去打球。"
},
{
  "id":"ASTRI06",
  "sentence":"大家討論緊這件事。"
}
```

the corresponding gold standard becomes:

```
{
  "id":"ASTRI05",
  "typo":null,
  "cantonese":null,
  "reorder":[
    {
      "position":1,
      "length":8,
      "correction":["我先走然後去打球"]
    }]
},
{
  "id":"ASTRI06",
  "typo":null,
  "cantonese":[
    {
      "position":5,
      "length":1,
      "correction":["正在"]
    }],
  "reorder":[
    {
      "position":1,
      "length":8,
      "correction":["大家緊討論這件事"]
    }]
}
```

3.2 Task 1 – Detection

Given a sentence, the system should be able to detect where the errors are, and for each detected error determine its type. Note that a sentence may have no errors, one error, or multiple errors (of multiple types).

3.3 Task 2 – Correction

For each detected error, the system should suggest how to correct the error. In contrast to previous similar computerised spelling check tasks (Duan et al., 2012; Tseng et al., 2015; Wu et al., 2013; Yu et al., 2008, 2014; Zhao and Liu, 2010), this shared task allows multiple correction suggestions. This idea originated from the fact that each spelling checker in modern word processing software provides a list of possible corrections for any given error, in order to maximise editing flexibility. Hence, it is reasonable to allow a system to output multiple correction suggestions for an error rather than just one.

4 Evaluation Schema

4.1 Evaluating Detection Performance

For evaluating the detection performance of a system, we compare the system output to the gold standard in terms of types of error and positions. Mathematically,

$$p = \frac{TP}{TP + FP}$$

$$r = \frac{TP}{TP + FN} \tag{1}$$

$$E_{detection} = \frac{2 \times p \times r}{p + r}$$

where TP is the number of characters that are correctly identified as errors; FP is the number of characters that are incorrectly identified as errors; and FN is the number of errors that remained undetected. For example, given the following sentences:

```
{
  "id":"ASTRI2000",
  "sentence":"佢想禾你共進免餐。"
},
{
  "id":"ASTRI2001",
  "sentence":"仍記得小學下課的時候，我總愛到
              草推裏捉蠶蟲。"
},
{
  "id":"ASTRI2002",
  "sentence":"我走先然後去打球。"
}
```

and the following result:

```
{
  "id":"ASTRI2000",
  "typo":[
    {
      "position":3,
      "correction":["和"]
    },
    {
      "position":7,
      "correction":["晚", "挽", "行"]
    }],
  "cantonese":[
    {
      "position":1,
      "length":1,
      "correction":["他", "她"]
    }],
  "reorder":[]
},
{
  "id":"ASTRI2001",
  "typo":[
    {
      "position":1,
      "correction":["也"]
    }],
  "cantonese":[],
  "reorder":[]
},
{
  "id":"ASTRI2002",
  "typo":[],
  "cantonese":[],
  "reorder":[]
}
```

then $TP = 3$ (detected the typos 禾 and 免; detected the Cantonese usage 佢), $FP = 1$ (incorrectly suggested 仍 as a typo in ASTRI2001), and $FN = 2$ (did not detect the typo 推 in ASTRI2001 and did not detect the ordering problem of AS-TRI2002).

4.2 Evaluating Correction Performance

There may be multiple ways to correct an error in a sentence. Hence, in the gold standard we included as many valid corrections as possible for each error. For example, given the following sentence:

```
{
  "id":"ASTRI2001",
  "sentence":"他想禾你共進免餐。"
}
```

the gold standard is:

```
{
  "id":"ASTRI2001",
  "typo":[
    {
```

```
      "position":3,
      "correction":["和"]
    },
    {
      "position":7,
      "correction":["晚", "午"]
    }],
  "cantonese":[],
  "reorder":[]
}
```

In this sentence 免 is a typo. Since 免 and 晚 have similar shapes whereas 免 and 午 have similar pronunciations, we consider both 晚 and 午 to be valid corrections of 免.

A correction in the gold standard is considered *successfully detected* when a system provided a correction suggestion for the same position. For every successfully detected error, a system is expected to deliver one or more appropriate correction suggestions. Consider the above example. If a system suggests a list of corrections [晚, 免] for position 7, then we evaluate that this system successfully detected the corresponding gold standard error, and that it provided one matching and one mismatching correction suggestion.

In order to avoid the case where a system provides long lists of correction suggestions in order to cover all gold standard corrections, a penalty proportional to the number of invalid provided suggestions is imposed. Mathematically,

$$E_{correction} = \frac{1}{|W|} \sum_{\forall i \in W} \frac{|G_i \cap U_i|}{|U_i|} \tag{2}$$

where W is the set containing all successfully detected errors; G_i is the set containing the gold standard suggestions for error $i \in W$; and U_i is the set containing the system correction suggestions for error $i \in W$. For G_i and U_i, major cases are:

- $G_i \cap U_i = G_i = U_i$:
  all system suggestions are in the gold standard corrections, and vice versa.

- $G_i \cap U_i = \emptyset$:
  no system suggestions are in the gold standard corrections.

- $G_i \cap U_i = U_i$ and $|G_i| \gneq |U_i|$:
  all system suggestions are in the gold standard corrections, but not all gold standard corrections are in the system suggestions.

- $G_i \cap U_i \neq \emptyset$ and $|G_i \cap U_i| \lneq |U_i|$:
  at least one system suggestion is in the gold

standard corrections, and at least one system suggestion is not in the gold standard corrections.

4.3 Evaluating Overall Performance

In practice, we usually need to obtain a single number to denote the reliability of a system. We suggest to use an evaluation schema similar to F_1 (Sebastiani, 2002):

$$E_{overall} = \frac{2 \times E_{detection} \times E_{correction}}{E_{detection} + E_{correction}} \qquad (3)$$

where $E_{detection}$ and $E_{correction}$ are obtained from Sections 4.1 and 4.2, respectively.

5 Discussion and Conclusion

We have seven registered participants from different organisations and universities, including Beijing University of Posts and Telecommunications, National Chia-Yi University, Peking University, and Harvard University. Upon receiving and reviewing the reports, we included the reports "Chinese Spelling Check based on N-gram and String Matching Algorithm" from National Chia-Yi University and "N-gram Model for Chinese Grammatical Error Diagnosis" from Beijing University of Posts and Telecommunications in this proceeding. These two universities used completely different approaches for detection and correction. In terms of results, National Chia-Yi University achieved a detection score of 42.71%, a correction score of 95.47%, and an overall system performance score of 59.01%, which is rather impressive. We encourage our readers to refer to their papers in order to fully appreciate the diversity of their approaches, with their specific advantages and drawbacks.

To conclude, this paper described the Chinese spelling check task at NLPTEA 2017. We illustrated the difficulties of Chinese spelling checking and how it is different from the alphabet-based languages. We released the first ever benchmark dataset which takes the colloquialism property into account, and we proposed a new evaluation schema. The main breakthrough, however, is that we allowed systems to provide multiple correction suggestions, which is a property of most commercial spelling checkers and desirable from the user's perspective, yet missing in existing evaluation schemas and still generally neglected in the research community.

We hope that this shared task will provide inspiration and motivation to advance our knowledge and experience regarding Chinese language processing in general, and to continue the development of state-of-the-art techniques for Chinese spelling checking in particular. We sincerely thank ASTRI and all participants in this shared task.

References

Huiming Duan, Zhifang Sui, Ye Tian, and Wenjie Li. 2012. The CIPS-SIGHAN CLP 2012 Chinese Word Segmentation on MicroBlog Corpora Bakeoff. In *Proceedings of the Second CIPS-SIGHAN Joint Conference on Chinese Language Processing (CLP 2012)*, pages 35–40.

Eric Mays, Fred J Damerau, and Robert L Mercer. 1991. Context Based Spelling Correction. *Information Processing & Management*, 27(5):517–522.

Fabrizio Sebastiani. 2002. Machine learning in automated text categorization. *ACM Computing Surveys (CSUR)*, 34(1):1–47.

Yuen-Hsien Tseng, Lung-Hao Lee, Li-Ping Chang, and Hsin-Hsi Chen. 2015. Introduction to SIGHAN 2015 Bake-off for Chinese Spelling Check. *ACL-IJCNLP 2015*, pages 32–37.

Shih-Hung Wu, Chao-Lin Liu, and Lung-Hao Lee. 2013. Chinese Spelling Check Evaluation at SIGHAN Bake-off 2013. In *Proceedings of the Seventh SIGHAN Workshop on Chinese Language Processing*, pages 35–42.

Liang-Chih Yu, Lung-Hao Lee, Yuen-Hsien Tseng, and Hsin-Hsi Chen. 2014. Overview of SIGHAN 2014 Bake-off for Chinese Spelling Check. In *Proceedings of the Third CIPS-SIGHAN Joint Conference on Chinese Language Processing (CLP 2014)*, pages 126–132.

Xiaofeng Yu, Wai Lam, Shing-Kit Chan, Yiu Kei Wu, and Bo Chen. 2008. Chinese NER Using CRFs and Logic for the Fourth SIGHAN Bakeoff. In *Proceedings of the Sixth SIGHAN Workshop on Chinese Language Processing*, pages 102–105.

Hongmei Zhao and Qun Liu. 2010. The CIPS-SIGHAN CLP 2010 Chinese Word Segmentation Bakeoff. In *Proceedings of the First CPS-SIGHAN Joint Conference on Chinese Language Processing*, pages 199–209.

Chinese Spelling Check based on
N-gram and String Matching Algorithm

Jui-Feng Yeh*, Li-Ting Chang, Chan-Yi Liu , Tsung-Wei Hsu

Department of Computer Science & Information Engineering,
National Chia-Yi University,
Chiayi city, Taiwan (R.O.C.)
{ralph, 1060416, 1060417, 1050480}@mail.ncyu.edu.tw

Abstract

This paper presents a Chinese spelling check approach based on language models combined with string match algorithm to treat the problems resulted from the influence caused by Cantonese mother tone. N-grams first used to detecting the probability of sentence constructed by the writers, a string matching algorithm called Knuth-Morris-Pratt (KMP) Algorithm is used to detect and correct the error. According to the experimental results, the proposed approach can detect the error and provide the corresponding correction.

1 Introduction

In recent years, Chinese became more and more popular. Not only the Asian learning it as a mother language, but also people around the world learning as the second language. But Chinese is not easy to learn for almost every kinds of people. Due to the diversity of Chinese characters and flexibility of grammars, Chinese spelling correction plays an important role in both foreign learners and Natural Language Processing researchers.

Traditional Chinese is a sophisticated art. With Cantonese, it could be even harder. The high-educated may sometimes spell it wrong, not to mention those who are learning it. Because of the following reasons, Traditional Chinese is more difficult to learn than other languages. First, the Chinese's grammar is more complicated and more flexible than English's. For Cantonese usage, the orderings of some characters are sometimes incor-

rect. Second, Chinese characters are evolved from by Hieroglyphic. Every single character has its own meanings, but two or more characters combined to a word can express a whole different meaning. Therefore, we can simply classify the errors to Typo, which is spelling error, Cantonese usage, and ordering error. In this paper, we proposed the Chinese spelling check with Cantonese correction system using N-gram language model and Knuth-Morris-Pratt (KMP) algorithm. It can detect the spelling error and Cantonese usage form a sentence, then give the suggested correction.

In NLP-TEA 2017, a share task for Chinese spelling check (CSC) aims to detect and correct the spell errors in text. There are three error types defined in Table 1. 'Typo' for spelling error, 'Cantonese' for only Cantonese usage, 'reorder' for incorrect order in Cantonese usage. Some typical examples of the errors are shown in Table 1. For this shared task, each input could have multiple errors, which means that it might need several phrases to process each input sentence. As the result of that, the proposed system is divided as two phrases, Preprocessing phrase and Chinese spelling check with Cantonese correction phrase.

Error types	Examples of erroneous sentences	Examples of correct sentences
拼字錯誤 (Typo)	我喜歡吃**梁**瓜炒蛋飯。	我喜歡吃**涼**瓜炒蛋飯。
粵語字詞 (Cantonese)	**佢**比你高	**他**比你高
語序錯誤 (Ordering)	我**走先**然後去打球	我**先走**然後去打球

Table 1: Some typical examples of the errors

Proceedings of the 4th Workshop on Natural Language Processing Techniques for Educational Applications, pages 35–38,
Taipei, Taiwan, December 1, 2017 ©2017 AFNLP

For each input sentence, the system should output the location, length, and the corresponding correction. In order to address the problem, we need to establish Cantonese to Traditional Chinese dictionary. NLP-TEA 2017 released a dictionary about 1000 words, then we according to an open traditional Chinese and Cantonese dictionary (http://kaifangcidian.com/han/yue) added up to 8000 words. Figure 1 shows the example of Cantonese usage errors detected by the proposed system and Figure 2 shows the example of typo error errors detected by the proposed system.

- Example 1
  Input：這個週末，我們全家去渡假村泡溫泉。
  Output：0

- Example 2
  Input：媽媽不停地催速我：「快點穿衣服！不然就趕不上校車了！」
  Output：1 19 1 便

- Example 3
  Input：她細聲地對我說：「我借你一枝鉛筆。」
  Output：1 2 2 小聲

- Example 4
  Input：我在雪糕店工作那時，我們曾招待外藉人士的家庭，他們成日光顧，可是我們不喜歡他們。
  Output：1 3 2 冰淇淋

- Example 5
  Input：為什麼所有人也蝕錢而主角可以賺錢？
  Output：1 8 2 虧本,虧錢

Figure 1: Examples of Cantonese usage errors output by proposed system

- Example 1
  Input：我們栽歌栽舞，歡慶新一年到來。
  Output：載 3 載 5

- Example 2
  Input：媽媽不停地催速我：「快點穿衣服！不然就趕不上校車了！」
  Output：促 7

- Example 3
  Input：每年的情人節，爸爸都會帶著他的朋友逛花店，碰巧就是媽媽工作的花店，爸爸會讓媽媽挑選最美麗的一束玫瑰花送給朋友。
  Output：玫 48

- Example 4
  Input：爺爺的農莊裏有一些小胡蘆，我常用它們來裝水。
  Output：葫 11

- Example 5
  Input：現代科技的發展日新月義，不斷進步。
  Output：異 11

Figure 2: Examples of Typo errors output by proposed system

This paper is organized as follows: Section 2 describe the proposed method of Chinese spelling check with Cantonese correction system. Section 3 we analyze the performance in experimental results of the proposed system. Finally, Section 4 the conclusion of this paper.

2 The Proposed Method

In this section, the processing flow is shown as follow. The proposed system is divided as two main phrases: Preprocessing phrase and Chinese spelling check with Cantonese correction phrase. In Pre-processing phrase, we first extracting the information from the data that NLP-TEA 2017 released. First CKIP (Chinese Knowledge and Information Processing) Auto tag was applied to do word segmentation and obtain part-of-speech(POS). Then we proceed to Chinese spelling check phrase. Based on the POS, we determine whether the words in the sentence is correct, detail will describe in section 2.1. In section 2.2, we will describe the process of Cantonese correction and the algorithm we applied.

2.1 Language Models for Error Checking

In this section, we will explain how the works, and the method we used for checking words in sentences.

Equation 1 is the possibility of a string of characters from N-gram language model. For example, a string "我(I) 吃了(ate) 漢堡(hamburger)", can obtain the possibility P(" 我 (I) 吃 了 (ate) 漢 堡 (hamburger)")is equal to the production of P("我(I)")P(" 吃 了 (ate)" | " 我 (I)") and P(" 漢 堡 (hamburger)" | "我(I) 吃了(ate)"). In which P("漢堡(hamburger)"|"我(I) 吃了(ate)"), "我(I)" "吃了(ate)" is the left context dependency of "漢堡(hamburger)". With this approach, we can count the word and calculate the words' possibility. Furthermore, use this possibility to measure whether the word is correct or not.

$$P(S) = P(w_1 w_2 \dots w_n)$$
$$= P(w_n | w_1 w_2 \dots w_{n-1}) P(w_1 w_2 \dots w_{n-1})$$
$$= P(w_n | w_1 w_2 \dots w_{n-1}) P(w_{n-1} | w_1 w_2 \dots w_{n-2}) P(w_1 w_2 \dots w_{n-2})$$
$$= P(w_1) \prod_{i=2}^{n} P(w_i | w_1 w_2 \dots w_{i-1})$$

Equation 1: Equation of the N-gram language model

After, we introduced the E-HowNet and a dictionary of Similar Pronunciation & Shape in Chinese character. We input the pre-processed data into proposed system, comparing with E-HowNet dictionary, processing flow shown as Figure 3.

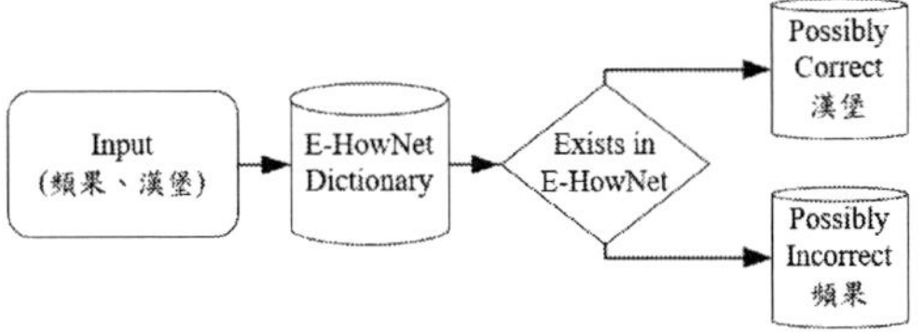

Figure 3: Example of comparing flow

With the collection of possibly incorrect words, we find the similar character from the dictionary of Similar Pronunciation & Shape in Chinese character to exchange the character in word separately. Then compare with E-HowNet dictionary again, if the exchanged word exists, means the exchanged word is correct and save it into a file.

The following Figure 4 shows an example of word exchanging, we exchange a character separately, then compare with E-HowNet dictionary, if the exchange result exists in E-HowNet, the process will stop and move on to the next word.

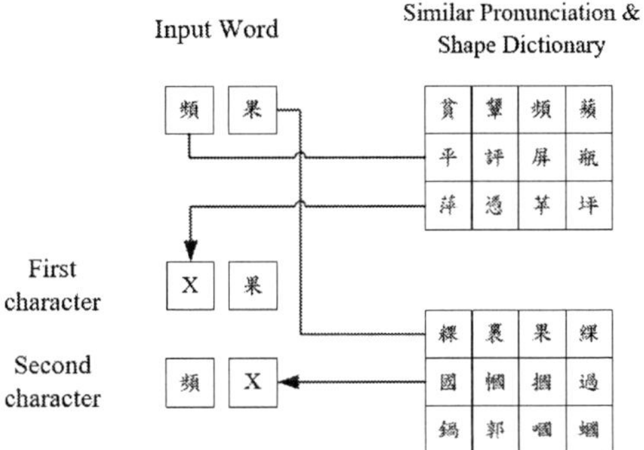

Figure 4: The exchange process of the word

2.2 Knuth-Morris-Pratt Algorithm for Correction

The correction system's main algorithm is based on KMP string matching algorithm. The KMP algorithm is used to search the specific string in a sentence. KMP is known for its highly effectiveness because it can search the specific string without starting over. In the middle of searching, we can also note down the position of the target string, which helps us to find out where the Cantonese usage is. Figure 5 shows an example of KMP algorithm, as the figure shows, we can skip lots of searching iteration.

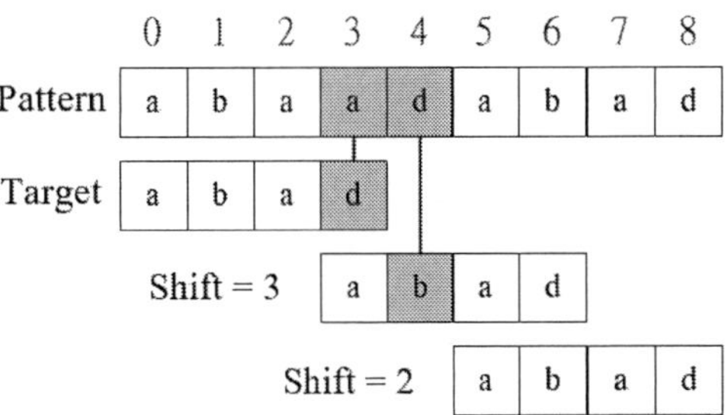

Figure 5: Example of KMP algorithm

When it comes to Cantonese correction, it is a lot easier than English string, because most of the Cantonese word are the combination of two or three character, word's length is often shorter than the English word.

By the using of KMP algorithm, any words that built in the dictionary appears in sentences, we will note the positon of the word and the translation of Cantonese usage. After search all the data, we will output a file that contain every result of the sentences, and according to this file output in the form of demanded format.

3 Experiments and Results

This experiment is based on the training data and testing data from NLP-TEA 2017. Each of the data contains 1000 sentences. After this experiment those sentences would be labeled with error tags and revise them or correct tags. And the results would determine by the performance standard given by NLP-TEA 2017 workshop. The evaluation matrices are shown as follow:

$$Precision = \frac{TP}{TP + FP} \quad (2)$$

$$Recall = \frac{TP}{TP + FN} \quad (3)$$

$$Performance_{Detection} = \frac{2*Precision*Recall}{Precision+Recall} \quad (4)$$

The confusion matrix is shown below in Table 2.

	System Results	
	Positive	Negative
Golden Standard Positive	TP (True Positive)	FP (False Negative)
Golden Standard Negative	FN (False Positive)	TN (True Negative)

Table 2: Confusion Matrix

Table 3 shows the detection performance evaluated by NLP-TEA 2017 workshop. TP, FP and FN are 243, 143, and 509 respectively. By the formulas above, we can obtain precision, recall and performance are 62.9534%, 32.3138% and 42.7065% respectively.

Metric	Value
TP	243
FP	143
FN	509
Precision	62.9534%
Recall	32.3138%
Performance	42.7065%

Table 3: Detection performance by proposed system

There are other two standards for evaluations given by NLP-TEA 2017 workshop, Correction Performance and Overall System Performance. Correction performance is for each detected error, contestants' system would deliver one or more (five at most) correction suggestions, if correction suggestions are correct means that the union between the golden standard suggestions and the contestants' suggestions is not null. Following is the formula for Correction performance,

$$Performance_{Correction} = \frac{1}{|W|} \sum_{\forall i \in w} \frac{|G_i \cap U_i|}{|U_i|} \quad (5)$$

Overall system performance means NLP-TEA 2017 ranked performance of the system as follows,

$$Performance_{Overall} = \frac{2 * Performance_{Detection} * (Performance_{Correction})}{(Performance_{Detection}) + Performance_{Correction}} \quad (6)$$

The result of proposed system evaluated by NLP-TEA 2017 is shown as follow:

Type	Value
Correction Performance	95.4737%
Overall System Performance	59.0149%

Table 4. Correction performance and overall system performance by our system

4 Conclusions

This paper main purpose is solving the NLP-TEA 2017 shared task for Chinese spelling check with Cantonese usage. Our proposed methods include KMP algorithm string matching and N-gram language model. According to the result of proposed system, it shows our system have some weakness should be revised. Recall rate is not ideal, it means that the proposed system should revised the algorithm of detecting Chinese spelling. But there is an advantage in the proposed system, the performance evaluation given by NLP-TEA 2017 shows that the correction performance of our system archives 95%. Therefore, we believe the proposed system is feasible. In the future, we will make an effort to improve the overall performance, especially on error detection to increase the recall rate.

References

CKIP AutoTag http://ckipsvr.iis.sinica.edu.tw/

E-HowNet http://ehownet.iis.sinica.edu.tw/

Rasool et al. 2012. Parallelization of KMP string matching algorithm on different SIMD architectures: Multi-core and GPGPU's. *International Journal of Computer Applications*, *49*(11).

Ku, D. T., and Chang, C. C. 2012. Development of context awareness learning system for elementary Chinese language learning. In *Genetic and Evolutionary Computing (ICGEC), 2012 Sixth International Conference*:538-541.

Lin, C. C., and Tsai, R. T. H. 2012. A Generative Data Augmentation Model for Enhancing Chinese Dialect Pronunciation Prediction. *IEEE Transactions on Audio, Speech, and Language Processing*, *20*(4):1109-1117.

Yeh et al. 2015. Condition Random Fields-based Grammatical Error Detection for Chinese as Second Language. In *Proceedings of The 2nd Workshop on Natural Language Processing Techniques for Educational Applications*:105-110.

Lee et al. 2016. Overview of NLP-TEA 2016 Shared Task for Chinese Grammatical Error Diagnosis. In *Proceedings of the 3rd Workshop on Natural Language Processing Techniques for Educational Applications (NLPTEA2016)*:40-48.

Matthews, S., and Yip, V. 2013. *Cantonese: A comprehensive grammar*. Routledge.

Kingsbury et al 2013. A high-performance Cantonese keyword search system. In *Acoustics, Speech and Signal Processing (ICASSP), 2013 IEEE International Conference*:8277-8281.

Cooper, A., and Wang, Y. 2012. The influence of linguistic and musical experience on Cantonese word learning. *The Journal of the Acoustical Society of America*, *131*(6):4756-4769.

Gao et al. 2000. Acoustic modeling for Chinese speech recognition: A comparative study of Mandarin and Cantonese. In *ICASSP'00. Proceedings. 2000 IEEE International Conference on* (Vol. 3): 1261-1264.

N-gram Model for Chinese Grammatical Error Diagnosis

Jianbo Zhao, Hao Liu, Zuyi Bao, Xiaopeng Bai[1], Si Li, Zhiqing Lin

Beijing University of Posts and Telecommunications, Beijing, China

[1]East China Normal University, Shanghai, China

{zhaojianbo, xiaohao_0033, baozuyi, lisi, linzq}@bupt.edu.cn,

xpbai@zhwx.ecnu.edu.cn

Abstract

Detection and correction of Chinese grammatical errors have been two of major challenges for Chinese automatic grammatical error diagnosis. This paper presents an N-gram model for automatic detection and correction of Chinese grammatical errors in NLPTEA 2017 task. The experiment results show that the proposed method is good at correction of Chinese grammatical errors.

1 Introduction

The goal of the NLPTEA 2017 shared task[1] for Chinese spelling check is to develop a computer-assisted system to automatically diagnose typing errors in Traditional Chinese sentences written by native Hong Kong primary students. Two kinds of errors are defined in the Chinese grammatical error diagnosis of NLPTEA 2017: typo and Cantonese usage. Typical error examples are shown in Table 1. In this NLPTEA task, the given sentences may not be wrong or not less than one error.

Spelling check is a common task for every language. It is an automatic mechanism to detect and correct spelling errors. An automatic spelling check system should have abilities about error detection and error correction. Error detection is to

Table 1: Typical error examples

Error Type	Error Sentence
No error	我很喜歡吃媽媽做的涼瓜炒蛋飯。 (I like to eat my mother's rice with balsam pear scrambled eggs)
Typo only	我很喜歡吃媽媽做的<u>梁</u>瓜炒蛋飯。
Cantonese usage only	我很<u>鍾意</u>吃媽媽做的涼瓜炒蛋飯。
Typo and Cantonese usage	我很<u>鍾意</u>吃媽媽做的<u>梁</u>瓜炒蛋飯。
Multiple typos and multiple Cantonese usages	我很<u>鍾意食</u>媽媽做的<u>梁</u>瓜炒<u>旦</u>飯。

find the various types of spelling errors in the text. And error correction is to replace some inappropriate words and characters by some reasonable ones.

With the close connection of mainland China and Hong Kong, it is essential for native Hong Kong primary students, who use Cantonese in their daily life, to learn some grammar and semantics of Mandarin Chinese. Additionally, as primary students, they can not avoid making some spelling mistakes like typos. Therefore, Chinese spelling check is becoming a significant task nowadays.

The same Chinese words express different meanings in different contexts. These are very difficult for beginners to master and challenge the establishment of automatic Chinese detection and correction system. Language modeling

[1]https://www.labviso.com/nlptea2017/

Proceedings of the 4th Workshop on Natural Language Processing Techniques for Educational Applications, pages 39–44,
Taipei, Taiwan, December 1, 2017 ©2017 AFNLP

(LM) (Goodman, 2001) is widely used in Chinese spelling check. The most widely-used and well-practiced language model, by far, is the N-gram LM (Wu et al., 2015), because of its simplicity and fair predictive power. Ensemble Learning (Xiang et al., 2015), CRF (Wu et al., 2015) and LSTM network (Shiue et al., 2017) have also been used in recent years to diagnose Chinese error.

Our work in this paper uses an N-gram LM to detect and correct possible spelling errors. And we also do word segmentation in a pre-processing stage which can improve the system performance. In our model, we first make word and character segmentation of the text. Second, the processed text is used as an input of the N-gram model, then the output K value is used to determine whether the word and character are wrong. If the word and character are wrong, the detection model will output the location and the length of the wrong word and character. Finally, output information of the detection model is used as an input of the correction model. The correction model outputs the correction information by matching and searching in the dictionaries.

This paper is organized as follows: Section 2 describes the N-gram model of the detection system we proposed for this task. Section 3 describes the error correction model we put forward for this task. Section 4 shows the data analysis and the evaluation results. Section 5 concludes this paper and illustrates the future work.

2 A Chinese Error Detection Model Based on N-gram

2.1 Introduction of the N-gram basic model

The N-gram model (Wu et al., 2001) is one of the most common mathematical models in natural language processing. It is defined as: the assumption sequence $W_1 W_2 \cdots W_n$ is a Markov chain, and then the probability of an element W_i is only related to the preceding N-1 elements:

$$P(W_i|W_1...W_{i-1}) = P(W_i|W_{i-n+1}...W_{i-1}) \quad (1)$$

Therefore, the N-gram model can be regarded as an N-1 Markov chain. According to Markov stochastic process, the probability of symbol string $S = W_1 W_2 \cdots W_n$ can be calculated by the initial probability distribution and the transfer probability as follows:

$$P(S) = P(W_1) \cdot \prod (P(W_k|W_{k-n+1}^{k-1})) \quad (2)$$

where $P(W_1)$ can be considered as an initial probability distribution and $P(W_k|W_{k-n+1}^{k-1})$ can be regarded as a state transition probability. W_{k-n+1}^{k-1} indicates $W_{k-n+1}W_{k-n+2}...W_{k-1}$.

It can be seen that the bigger the N is, the closer the word order is to the real word, which produces better results. However, in practical application, the growth of the N not only causes the number of parameters increases sharply, but also brings some evaluation errors. So in actual use, we only consider the situation when N=1,N=2,N=3, namely Unigram, Bigram and Trigram (Liu et al., 2011).

2.2 A model of word continuous relation judgment

This model is used to determine whether characters or words continue to occur incorrectly, such as a sentence $S = Z_1 Z_2 \cdots Z_i Z_{i+1} \cdots Z_m$. $Z_i Z_{i+1}$ are two consecutive characters or words. By using the probability model of two characters or words, we check the target character or word, so as to determine whether the character or word is correct. In other words, if the character or word is correct, it can only be judged by its continuous relationship with the character or word.

Take Bigram as an example, in order to check whether Z_i is error, we just need to check the adjacent relations of Z_{i-1} and Z_i, if Z_{i-1} to Z_i transfer probability $P(Z_i|Z_{i-1})$ meets a certain threshold condition, then we consider Z_{i-1} and Z_i are continuous, otherwise we think Z_{i-1} and Z_i are not continuous, then we consider Z_i is error.

$$P(Z_{i-1}) = \frac{R(Z_{i-1})}{N} \qquad (3)$$

$$P(Z_i) = \frac{R(Z_i)}{N} \qquad (4)$$

$P(Z_{i-1})$ is the probability of Z_{i-1} in training corpus, and $P(Z_i)$ is the probability of Z_i in training corpus. $R(Z_{i-1})$ represents the number of occurrences of Z_{i-1} in the entire training corpus. $R(Z_i)$ represents the number of occurrences of Z_i in the entire training corpus. N represents the total number of strings in the training corpus.

$$P(Z_{i-1}, Z_i) = \frac{R(Z_{i-1}, Z_i)}{N} \qquad (5)$$

$P(Z_{i-1}, Z_i)$ represents the probability of continuity of Z_{i-1} and Z_i. $R(Z_{i-1}, Z_i)$ indicates the total number of consecutive occurrences of Z_{i-1} and Z_i in the training corpus.

So the condition of judging whether Z_{i-1} and Z_i is continuous is $R(Z_{i-1}, Z_i) \geq \tau_0$. If $R(Z_{i-1}, Z_i) \geq \tau_0$ is established, then we consider Z_{i-1} and Z_i are continuous, otherwise we consider Z_i is wrong.

2.3 A model of error detection based on different N-gram models

In this NLPTEA task, we use different N-gram models to determine whether the text is wrong or not. From the above mentioned, we know that model based on N-gram needs to have the frequency of characters and words. Through large corpus, we can construct the Bigram model, the Trigram model of characters and words and characters and words frequency table.

The corpus we use is middle and primary school texts organized by East China Normal University that has been made Chinese word segmentation.

For the Unigram model, we need to count the number of occurrences of each character and word in the corpus. For example, the number of occurrences of W_i is C_i, the probability of W_i is

$$P(W_i) = \frac{C_i}{N} \qquad (6)$$

For the Bigram model, we need to count the number of continuous occurrences of two characters and words in the corpus. For example, the number of continuous occurrences of W_i and W_{i-1} is $C_{i-1,i}$.

$$P(W_i|W_{i-1}) = \frac{C_{i-1,i}}{C_{i-1}} \qquad (7)$$

For the Trigram model, we need to count the number of continuous occurrences of three characters and words in the corpus. For example, the number of continuous occurrences of W_{i-2}, W_{i-1} and W_i is $C_{i-2,i-1,i}$.

$$P(W_i|W_{i-1}W_{i-2}) = \frac{C_{i-2,i-1,i}}{C_{i-2,i-1}} \qquad (8)$$

$$P(W_i|W_{i-1}W_{i-2}) = \frac{C_{i-2,i-1,i}}{C_{i-2,i-1}} \qquad (9)$$

So we can get the detection model, including the character model, the word model, the Bigram model of characters and words, the Trigram model of characters and words.

The model of errors detection is shown in Figure 1.

2.4 Examples and parameters

Take the sentence "表演完了，空中的濃煙散開了，回復原來的消晰。" as an example, to check whether there is an error with "回復". After making Chinese word segmentation, the sentence is "表演/完/了/a/空中/的/濃煙/散/開/了/a/回復/原來/的/消晰/a". "a" presents a space. Examples of inputs of each model are shown in Table 2.

We use LTP model (Wanxiang Che, 2010) to make Chinese word segmentation. Since LTP

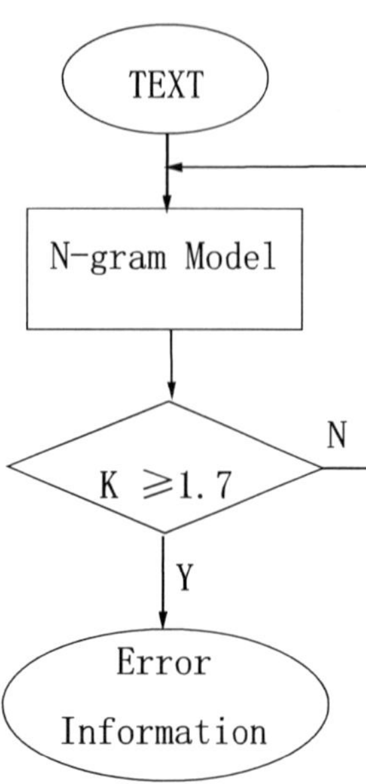

Figure 1: The Model of Errors Detection

The Model	Input Strings
The character Model	< 回>
The word Model	< 回復>
The Bigram model of words	<a, 回復> <回復,原來>
The Trigram model of words	< 了, a, 回復> < a,回復,原來> <回復,原來,的>
The Bigram model of characters	< a, 回> <回,復>
The Trigram model of characters	< 了, a,回> < a, 回,復> < 回,復, 原>

Table 2: Inputs of each model

is a model to segment simplified Chinese words, we first turn the traditional Chinese into simplified Chinese and then make word segmentation.

The character model: we take the text of characters as inputs and check whether the character exists in the dictionary of characters. If the character does not exist, $K = K + 2$, otherwise, the K value remains unchanged.

The word model: we take the text of words as inputs and check whether the word exists in the dictionary of words. If the word does not exist, $K = K + 2.7$, otherwise, the K value remains unchanged.

The Bigram model of words: we take the text of two consecutive words as inputs and check whether the two consecutive words exist in the dictionary of two consecutive words. If the two words do not exist, $K = K + 0.9$, otherwise, if the number of appearance is less than 3 times, $K = K + 0.2$, otherwise, $K = K - 1.2$.

The Trigram model of words: we take the text of three consecutive words as inputs and check whether the three consecutive words exist in the dictionary of three consecutive words. If the three words do not exist, $K = K + 0.4$, otherwise, $K = K - 1.2$.

The Bigram model of characters: we take the text of two consecutive characters as inputs and check whether the two consecutive characters exist in the dictionary of two consecutive characters. If the two characters do not exist, $K = K + 1$, otherwise, if the number of appearance is less than 3 times, otherwise, $K = K - 1.5$.

The Trigram model of characters: we take the text of three consecutive characters as inputs and check whether the three consecutive characters exist in the dictionary of three consecutive characters. If the three characters do not exist, $K = K + 0.3$, otherwise, $K = K - 1$.

After the above calculation, we get the K value, length and position of each character. The K value is used to determine whether it is wrong, and $length$ is used to indicate the length of wrong string, and $position$ refers to the start position of the wrong character in the sentence. If the K value is greater than 1.7, we consider the character and the word are wrong. The threshold value is determined by the combined effect of the above model.

Metric	Input Value
TP	88
FP	571
FN	664
Precision	13.3536%
Recall	11.7021%
Performance	12.4734%

Table 3: Detection Performance

Type	Input Value
Performance	90.9102%

Table 4: Correction Performance

3 Chinese Error Correction Model

$Similar prounciation$ and $Similar shape$ (Lee et al., 2015) are two dictionaries which are used to find similar characters and words in pronunciation and shape.

Corresponding to the two dictionaries, $Similar prounciation$ and $Similar shape$, we get the candidate sets SP_w and SS_w of the wrong character and word h_w respectively. SP_w refers to the elements of the set that has the similar pronunciation of h_w and SS_w refers to the elements of the set that has the similar shape of h_w. Then we concatenate SP_w and SS_w into a set called S_w. For $\forall s \in S$, we replace h_w by s into the original sentence, then we use 2-gram, 3-gram and 4-gram around the specific character, and we can collect 9 items for each character of specific position, including 2 items of 2-gram, 3 items of 3-gram and 4 items of 4-gram. We compare and sort the frequency of the 9 items in the word frequency dictionary W. We assume that after replacing, if some items are in dictionaries, the item which has more characters will have a higher probability to be the target choice. For example, the frequency of the item "和蔼" is 5, the frequency of the item "和蔼可亲" is 2. But if the second one appears in your candidate sets, it will have a higher probability than the first one

Type	Input Value
Performance	21.9370%

Table 5: Overall Performance

as we can imagine, so we can distribute different proportions to different types in dictionaries. Finally the most probable character is selected for eventual replacement.

When $length$ is higher than 1, we should replace the character from the start position to end position. End position is the plus of $position$ and $length$. Therefore, there should be multiple characters to be replaced at the same time, such as when $length$ is equal to 3, we replace the character in the $position$, the second and the third character that begin with $position$, all these three characters need to be replaced at the same time successively. Then we compare the frequency of all items. The comparison method is as above.

4 Result Analysis

The system results we obtained are shown in Table 3, Table 4 and Table 5. We can see from the results that the detection performance is not very well. The reason may be that the parameters of the complex N-gram model are not easy to control and to adjust. The results also show that the method we proposed is good at correction of Chinese grammatical errors and achieves a high accuracy.

5 Conclusion and Future Work

In this paper, we present an N-gram model for automatic detection and correction of Chinese grammatical errors. As we can see from the results, the performance of correction of Chinese grammatical errors is pretty good. In the future, we plan to employ neural network to Chinese grammatical error diagnosis.

6 Acknowledgements

This work was supported by Beijing Natural Science Foundation (4174098), National Natural Science Foundation of China (61702047) and the Fundamental Research Funds for the Central Universities (2017RC02).

References

Joshua T. Goodman. 2001. A bit of progress in language modeling. *Computer Speech & Language* 15(4):403–434.

Lung Hao Lee, Liang Chih Yu, and Li Ping Chang. 2015. Overview of the nlp-tea 2015 shared task for chinese grammatical error diagnosis. In *Overview of the NLP-TEA 2015 Shared Task for Chinese Grammatical Error Diagnosis*.

C. L. Liu, M. H. Lai, K. W. Tien, Y. H. Chuang, S. H. Wu, and C. Y. Lee. 2011. Visually and phonologically similar characters in incorrect chinese words:analyses, identification, and applications. *Acm Transactions on Asian Language Information Processing* 10(2):1–39.

Yow Ting Shiue, Hen Hsen Huang, and Hsin Hsi Chen. 2017. Detection of chinese word usage errors for non-native chinese learners with bidirectional lstm. In *Meeting of the Association for Computational Linguistics*. pages 404–410.

Zhenghua Li Ting Liu Wanxiang Che. 2010. Ltp: A chinese language technology platform. In *Coling 2010:Demonstrations*. pages 13–16.

Shih Hung Wu, Po Lin Chen, Liang Pu Chen, Ping Che Yang, and Ren Dar Yang. 2015. Chinese grammatical error diagnosis by conditional random fields. In *The Workshop on Natural Language Processing Techniques for Educational Applications*. pages 7–14.

Y. Wu, G. Wei, and H. Li. 2001. Word segmentation algorithm for chinese language based on n-gram models and machine learning. *Journal of Electronics & Information Technology* .

Yang Xiang, Xiaolong Wang, Wenying Han, and Qinghua Hong. 2015. Chinese grammatical error diagnosis using ensemble learning. In *The Workshop on Natural Language Processing Techniques for Educational Applications*. pages 99–104.

The Influence of Spelling Errors on Content Scoring Performance

Andrea Horbach, Yuning Ding, Torsten Zesch
Language Technology Lab,
Department of Computer Science and Applied Cognitive Science,
University of Duisburg-Essen, Germany
{andrea.horbach|torsten.zesch}@uni-due.de
yuning.ding@stud.uni-due.de

Abstract

Spelling errors occur frequently in educational settings, but their influence on automatic scoring is largely unknown. We therefore investigate the influence of spelling errors on content scoring performance using the example of the short answer data set of the Automated Student Assessment Prize (ASAP). We conduct an annotation study on the nature of spelling errors in the ASAP dataset and utilize these finding in machine learning experiments that measure the influence of spelling errors on automatic content scoring. Our main finding is that scoring methods using both token and character n-gram features are robust against spelling errors up to the error frequency seen in ASAP.

1 Introduction

Spelling errors occur frequently in educational assessment situations, not only in language learning scenarios, but also with native speakers, especially when answers are written without the help of a spell-checker.[1] In automatic content scoring for short answer questions, a model is learnt about which content needs to be present in a correct answer. Spelling mistakes interfere with this process, as they should be mostly ignored for content scoring. It is still largely unknown how severe the problem is in a practical setting.

Consider the following answer to the first prompt of the short answer data set of the Automated Student Assessment Prize (ASAP):[2]

(1)   *Some additional information you will need are the material. You also need to know the size of the **contaneir** to measure how the acid rain **effected** it. You need to know how much **vineager** is used for each sample. Another thing that would help is to know how big the sample stones are by **measureing** the best possible way.*

In this answer, three non-word spelling errors (printed in bold) occur. In addition, there is also one real-word spelling error, which leads to an existing word: *effected*, which should be *affected*.

While a teacher who is manually scoring learner answers can simply try to ignore spelling mistakes as far as possible, automatic scoring methods must include a spell-checking component to normalize an occurrence of *vineager* to *vinegar*. Thus spell-checking components are also a part of some content scoring systems, such as the top two performing systems in the ASAP challenge (Tandalla, 2012; Zbontar, 2012). However, it is unclear what impact spelling errors really have on the performance of content scoring systems.

Many systems in the ASAP challenge, as well as some participating systems in the SemEval 2013 Student Response Analysis Task (Heilman and Madnani, 2013; Levy et al., 2013), used shallow features such as token n-grams (Zbontar, 2012; Conort, 2012). If a token in the test data is misspelled, then there is no way of knowing that it has the same meaning as the correct spelling of the word in the training data. At the same time, individual spelling error instances are often not occurring uniquely in a dataset: Depending on factors such as the learner group (for example native speakers or language learners with a certain native language) or the data collection method (handwriting vs. typing) some spelling errors will occur frequently while others will be rare. The mis-

---

[1] Note that we do not distinguish between the terms *error* and *mistake* used by Ellis (1994) to denote competence and performance errors respectively. We use the two terms interchangeably.

[2] https://www.kaggle.com/c/asap-sas

45

Proceedings of the 4th Workshop on Natural Language Processing Techniques for Educational Applications, pages 45–53,
Taipei, Taiwan, December 1, 2017 ©2017 AFNLP

spelled form *vineger*, for example, might be frequent enough that an occurrence feature for the misspelled version provides valuable information which a classifier can learn. Whether this observation mitigates the effect of spelling errors depends on the frequency of individual errors and therefore also on the shape of error distributions.

Contributions   In this paper, we investigate how the presence or absence of spelling errors influences the task of content scoring, taking the afore-mentioned influence criteria of error frequency and error distribution into account. We conduct our analyses and experiments on the frequently used ASAP content scoring dataset (Higgins et al., 2014). The dataset contains 10 different prompts about different topics ranging from sciences over biology to literature questions. Each prompt comes with 2,200 answers on average. Although this dataset has been used in a lot of studies concerning content scoring, much about the spelling errors in the dataset is still unknown. Our manual annotations and corpus analyses will therefore also provide insight on the number, the nature and the distribution of spelling errors in this dataset.

First, we present an analysis of the frequency and distribution of non-word spelling errors in the ASAP corpus and compare several spelling dictionaries. We provide a gold-standard correction for the non-word errors found automatically by a spell checker in the test section of the data. We compare error correction methods based on phonetic and edit distance and extend them with a domain-specific method that prefers suggestions occurring in the material for a specific prompt.

Next, we investigate the effect of manipulating the number and distribution of spelling errors on the performance of an automatic content scoring system. We experiment with two ways of regulating the number of misspellings. We automatically and manually spell check the corpus to replace non-word spelling errors by their corrected version. This only allows us to decrease the number of errors. To increase the amount of spelling errors further, we also introduce errors artificially in two conditions: (i) adding random noise as a worst-case scenario, and (ii) adding mistakes according to the error distribution in the test data.

We find that token and character n-gram scoring features are largely robust against spelling errors with a frequency present in our data. Character n-gram features are contributing towards this robustness. When introducing more errors, we see a substantial drop in performance, such that the importance of spell-checking components in content scoring depends on the frequency of errors in the data.

2   Annotating Spelling Errors

In order to evaluate the influence of spelling errors on content scoring, we need an error-annotated corpus. However, a full manual annotation of the complete dataset, which contains around one million tokens, was beyond our means. Instead, we decided to annotate a representative sample of the ASAP corpus which we utilize to evaluate the performance of spelling error detection methods. This allows us to estimate whether we can draw reliable conclusions from applying existing spell checking methods to the full dataset.

We manually annotated the first 20 answers in each prompt using WebAnno (Yimam et al., 2013). In order to facilitate the annotation process, we automatically pre-annotate potential spelling errors using the Jazzy spelling dictionary.[3] Two annotators (non-native speakers and two of the authors of this paper) reviewed the error candidates and either accepted or rejected them, but could also mark additional spelling errors which were not detected automatically.

In this manual annotation process, we distinguish between non-word and real-word spelling errors. We annotate a mistake as real-word error if another word with a different root is clearly intended in the context, such as "*Their* are two samples". We do not distinguish between spelling errors and grammatical errors among the non-word errors, i.e., we do not filter out non-words that could originate from grammatical errors such as incorrect 3rd person forms like *dryed* instead of *dried*. We do not mark grammatical errors that lead to a real-word error, such as wrong prepositions. Equally, we do not mark lexically unsuitable words which are morphologically possible, but do not fit in the context, such as *counter partner* in a context where *counter part* was clearly intended.

In total, we annotated 9,995 tokens and reach an inter-annotator agreement of 0.87 Cohen's kappa (Cohen, 1960) on the binary decision whether a

---

[3] `https://sourceforge.net/projects/jazzy/files/Dictionaries/English/english.0.zip/download`

word is a spelling mistake or not. Main sources of disagreement were (i) misses of real word spelling errors not marked in the pre-annotation (e.g. *koala beer*), and (ii) disagreements as to whether compounds may be written as one word or not (e.g. *micro debris* vs. *microdebris*), a decision which is often ambiguous. In case of disagreement between the annotators, the final decision is made through adjudication by both annotators.

The resulting dataset contains 297 spelling errors, including 48 real-word errors which will not be considered for further evaluations and experiments. The resulting ratio of spelling errors in the dataset is about 3%, which is in line with the expected frequency of spelling errors in human-typed text (Kukich, 1992). However, it would be an interesting follow-up work to determine the frequency of spelling errors in other content scoring datasets.

2.1 Evaluating Automatic Spell-checking

Using our annotated answers, we now evaluate different spell-checking dictionaries. Note that the size and quality of those dictionaries influence the trade-off between precision and recall of error detection. For example, a very small dictionary yields almost perfect recall, as most spelling errors are not in the dictionary and flagged accordingly. However, precision would be rather low as some of the detected errors are perfectly valid words that are just missing from the dictionary. On the other hand, a very large dictionary lowers recall as some words that are definitely a spelling error in the context of the writing task in this dataset might be valid words in some very special context. For example, the HunSpell dictionary contains the abbreviation *AZT*, standing among others for 'azi-dothymidine' and 'Azerbaijan time'. In the context of our learner answers, the string would likely never occur as a valid word, but would be counted as a non-word misspelling.

In order to find a suitable dictionary for our task, we evaluate the following setups: As baseline dictionary, we use the one that comes with the **Jazzy** spell checker.[4] It is relatively small (about 47,000 entries) and does not contain inflected forms (such as third person singular). Thus, we also use the English **HunSpell** dictionary with more than 120,000 entries.[5] Both are general

Dictionary	P	R	F
Jazzy	.25	.98	.39
HunSpell	.63	.89	.74
HunSpell -abbr	.63	.95	.76
HunSpell +prompt	**.88**	.88	.88
HunSpell -abbr +prompt	.86	**.94**	**.90**

Table 1: Evaluation of different error detection dictionaries

purpose dictionaries, which we can adapt in order to get better performance. First, we remove all-uppercase abbreviations from the dictionary (**-abbr**), as they can lead to the above-mentioned problem.[6] Second, we extend the dictionary with prompt-specific lexical material (**+prompt**), which we extract automatically from the reading material and scoring rubrics associated with each prompt. This step adds about 600 tokens to the dictionary. Third, we combine both strategies (**-abbr +prompt**), keeping a word if it is contained both in the list of abbreviations and in the prompt material.

After checking the first results, we found that some artifacts influence the results. First, the tokenizer splits words like *can't* into two tokens *ca* and *n't*, which are then detected as spelling errors. Second, the learner answers often contain bullets used in lists, such as *a)*, *b)*, etc. For the final results, we do not count these cases as spelling errors.

Results Table 1 gives an overview of the results. As expected, the rather small Jazzy dictionary has very high recall as many words are not found in the dictionary, including almost all spelling errors but also a lot of valid words, which results in low precision. Using the larger HunSpell dictionary lowers recall a bit, but dramatically improves precision. Excluding abbreviations has less effect than expected. It might even hurt a bit, if words such as *DNA* are removed, which are frequently used in the biology prompts. Extending the dictionary with the small number of prompt-specific terms brings large boosts in detection precision with an – in comparison – moderate drop of recall. Excluding the abbreviations before adding the prompt-specific terms recovers most of the lost

---

[4]http://jazzy.sourceforge.net
[5]https://sourceforge.net/projects/
hunspell/files/Spelling%20dictionaries/
en_US/

[6]Note that in our experiments, we lowercase all material before the comparison so that we factor out capitalization problems.

recall and trades in some precision, but yields the best F-score.

It might be surprising that we do not reach a perfect recall in error detection, i.e. that there are words in the dictionary which we mark as incorrect. These include tokens from the prompt material which were annotated as incorrect (such as *microdebris* instead of *micro debris*), as well as erroneously tokenized words such as *a ddition* where both parts have been marked as part of a non-word spelling error although *a* appears in the dictionary.

Hunspell -abbr +prompt gives us overall the best performance and is thus used in the following experiments.

3 Annotating Error Corrections

In order to evaluate the performance of error correction methods, we manually correct part of the data. We use the **Hunspell -abbr +prompt** dictionary with the Jazzy spell-checker to detect and correct all errors in the test data part of ASAP. A list of these errors and their corrections are then presented to two human annotators (the same as in the previous annotation task). We showed each instance within a 20 character window to the left and right to allow for a decision in context, but annotators could inspect the full learner answer if that window was not sufficient. Annotators performed two consecutive tasks: First they accepted or rejected a word as a spelling error, thus sorting out words that should not have been flagged as an error in the first place. Next, they either accepted a proposed correction or changed it to a different one.

This approach was much less time consuming than performing manual error detection and correction on raw data, and allowed us to annotate the complete test data section of the corpus with 6,400 proposed error candidates. As the recall of the error detection approach is expected to be around 90-95% (see evaluation results in Table 1), we will miss some errors. However, we decided that an imperfect annotation of the full test data section is more useful than an almost perfect annotation of only parts of the answers.

For prompts 1 and 2, two annotators checked all instances on the training as well as on the test data. On these items, annotators reached an inter-annotator agreement of κ=0.90 on the decision whether a word should be considered an error. For those candidates considered an error by both annotators, they found the same correction in 86% of all cases. In addition, the test data for all 10 prompts was annotated by one annotator each. On this data, out of 6,400 error candidates, about 5,200 were accepted as errors. The resulting error detection precision of 81% is close to the values shown in Table 1.

There was a surprisingly high number of errors for which it was not possible to annotate a correction, because the answer was so garbled that annotators could not find a target hypothesis. An example for such a sentence is the following: *[...] but they don;t tell me to subtract the end mass from the slurhnf.* When looking at the wider context, it is somewhat plausible that *slurhnf* should be something along the lines of *start mass*, it remains unclear what the student meant. We checked some of these candidates with a native speaker, but still remained with almost 3% of uncorrectable errors. We ignore these cases when we evaluate different spell-checkers.

3.1 Evaluating Automatic Error Correction

We compare four setups of error correction methods. As a baseline, we use the original Jazzy spellchecker[7], which only generates candidates with the same phonetic code using **Metaphone** encoding. If there is more than one candidate, we select one randomly.

As a variant to random error candidate selection, we additionally use prompt knowledge (**+prompt**), i.e. we make use of the prompt material and of the frequency of words and bigrams in all answers for a prompt. We prefer material occurring in the prompt of an answer, if there are several candidates, we take the one occurring most frequently in the data. We observed in our annotations that a number of identified errors (1,065) are the result of tokenization errors on the side of the students, i.e. they often omit whitespace between two words. Often these errors evolve around punctuation marks (e.g. *content.they*), in which cases they are easy to detect and correct. In cases without punctuation showing the token boundary, we check whether an unknown word can be split into two in-dictionary words and accept the candidate if the resulting bigram also occurs in the answers for that prompt.

We also built our own spellchecker, which does not only take phonetically identical candidates

---

[7] http://sourceforge.net/projects/jazzy

into account, but all candidates up to a certain **Levenshtein** distance (3 was an optimal value in our case) using LibLevenshtein[8] for an efficient implementation, but prefers candidates with a shorter distance if possible. In analogy to the *Metaphone* setup, we test (i) a basic version where a candidate is randomly selected should several occur and (ii) a prompt-specific version.

Table 2 shows correction accuracy of the different methods on the annotated gold-standard, i.e. we check how often the correction method found the same correction as annotated, ignoring capitalization and ignoring words we could not manually correct. We also show coverage values, which specify for how many gold standard errors the respective method was able to provide a correction candidate at all. For our following experiments, we select the best-performing **Levenshtein +prompt** method.

Method	Variant	acc	coverage
Jazzy	Metaphone	.51	.85
Jazzy	Metaphone +prompt	.55	.82
Our	Levenshtein	.46	.96
Our	Levenshtein +prompt	**.69**	.95

Table 2: Performance of different error correction methods

4 Dataset Analysis

To get a better understanding of the nature of spelling errors, we provide additional analyses on our annotations.

4.1 Error Detection Analysis

For the error detection annotations, we compare the length of a token in characters to its likelihood of being misspelled and find that longer words have higher chances to be misspellings (see Figure 1).

To further drill down on the nature of errors we compute the probability of spelling errors across different coarse-grained POS tags. We map the Penn Treebank tagset to 12 coarse-grained tags as described in (Petrov et al., 2011). Table 3 shows that error occur mainly in content words (only 17 out of 255 annotated errors occur in function words).

Next, we investigate, how many errors are automatically detected in ASAP using the best performing dictionary. Table 4 provides an overview of the frequency of errors for each prompt, as well as the type-token-ratio for error tokens. We see that many errors occur more than once, which might have consequences for content scoring if a model is able to associate frequent misspellings with a certain label. Table 5 shows as an example the top 10 most frequent misspellings for prompt 2. We see that there are a few very frequent misspellings centered around important vocabulary for that prompt and a long tail of infrequent misspellings (not shown in the table).

We also check whether there is a correlation between the number of spelling errors in an answer and the content score assigned by a teacher. We normalize by the number of tokens in the answer to avoid length artifacts and find no significant correlation. This is in line with our general assumption that spelling errors are ignored by teachers when scoring a learner answer.

4.2 Error Correction Analysis

In order to understand the nature of spelling mistakes better, we perform additional analyses on the

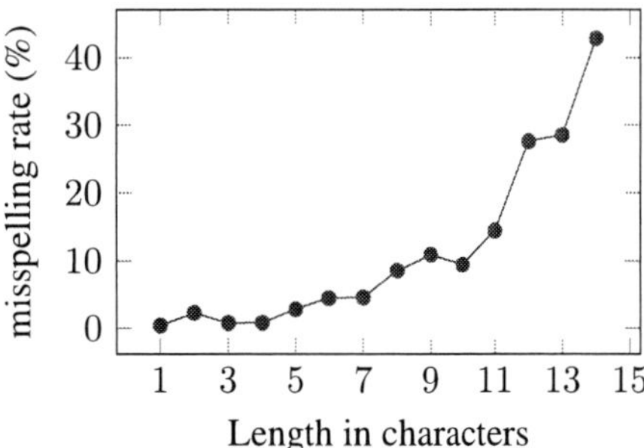

Figure 1: Probability for words of a certain length to be misspelled in our annotated data

POS	# instances	P(error|POS)
.	1	0.1
ADJ	26	4.2
ADP	5	0.5
ADV	27	4.8
CONJ	-	-
DET	3	0.3
NOUN	140	6.2
NUM	-	-
PRON	3	0.4
PRT	1	0.3
VERB	45	2.2
X	4	0.2

Table 3: Probability for tokens from a certain POS class to be misspelled.

---

[8]https://github.com/
universal-automata/liblevenshtein-java

prompt	# errors	TTR
1	1.2	.69
2	1.2	.64
3	1.0	.62
4	2.0	.51
5	7.7	.43
6	5.8	.62
7	1.5	.63
8	2.3	.42
9	2.1	.59
10	2.2	.43
∅	2.3	.56

Table 4: Average number of spelling mistakes per 100 tokens (punctuation excluded) and type-token-ratio for errors for the individual ASAP prompts.

Misspelling	#
streched	117
strech	31
strechable	18
nt	16
streching	15
expirement	13
streached	10
expiriment	9
strechiest	8
streches	6

Table 5: Top-10 most frequent misspellings for prompt 2

corrected test data. First, we categorized errors according to the Levenshtein distance between an error and its corrected version (see Figure 2). A number of instances with very high distances originate from errors involving tokenization, e.g. several words concatenated without a whitespace. To avoid such artifacts in the analysis, we counted only cases where both the original token and its corrected version did not include any whitespace.

There is still a surprisingly high number of words with a Levenshtein distance greater than 1. An example for a word with a high Levenshtein distance would be *satalight* instead of *satellite*. This shows that finding the right correction can be a challenging task, as correction candidates with a lower distance often exist. For example, in the answer *The students could have impared the experiment by (. . .)*, it becomes clear from the question context (*Describe two ways the student could have improved the experimental design*) that the right correction for *impared* is *improved* and not *impaired*.

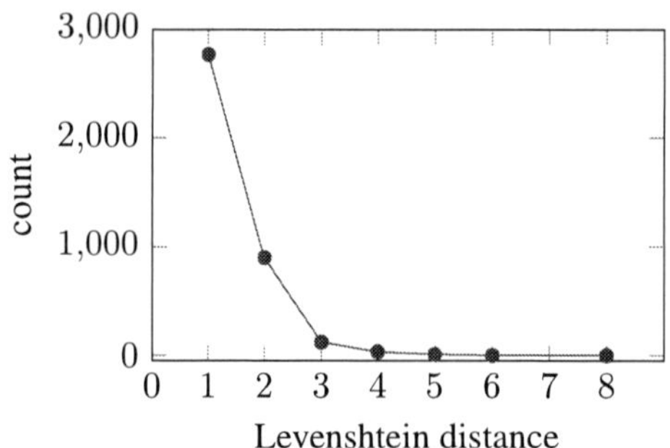

Figure 2: Distribution of errors across different Levenshtein distances.

5 Influence of Spelling Errors on Scoring

In the following experiments, we vary the amount of spelling errors in the data systematically. We use automatic and manual spell-checking to decrease the error rate and add artificial errors for a higher number of errors.

5.1 Experimental Setup

In our experimental studies, we examine the influence of spelling deviations and spell-checking on content scoring. We train one classification model for each of the ten ASAP prompts, using the published data split into training data and "public leaderbord" data for testing. We preprocess the data using the ClearNLP segmenter and POS tagger provided through DKPro Core (Eckart de Castilho and Gurevych, 2014). We use a standard feature set often used in content scoring (Higgins et al., 2014) and extract token 1–3 grams and character 2–4 grams using the top 10,000 most frequent n-grams in each feature group. We then train a SVM classifier (Hall et al., 2009) with default parameter settings provided through DKPro TC (Daxenberger et al., 2014). We evaluate using both accuracy and quadratically weighted kappa (QWK, Cohen (1968)), as proposed in the Kaggle competition for this dataset and present results averaged across all 10 prompts.

One important property of this feature setup is that the character n-gram features could be able to cover useful information from misspelled words. If the word *experiment* is, for example, misspelled as *expirment*, there are n-grams shared between these two versions, such as the character trigrams *exp*, *men* or *ent*. Therefore, we also use a reduced feature set, where we only work with token n-gram features, in order to quantify the size of this effect.

	tokens & chars		tokens only	
	QWK	acc	QWK	acc
baseline	.68	.71	.66	.70
spell-check train	.66	.70	.66	.70
spell-check test	.68	.70	.66	.70
spell-check both	.68	.70	.66	.70
gold test	.68	.70	.66	.70

Table 6: Scoring performance on ASAP with and without spell checking

# errors	# test items	QWK	acc
≥ 0	522	.66	.70
≥ 1	269	.65	.69
≥ 2	132	.63	.68
≥ 3	52	.62	.70

Table 7: Scoring performance on ASAP when using only answers with a certain minimal number of errors for testing.

5.2 Experiment 1 – Decreased Error Frequency

In a first machine learning experiment, we investigate the influence of spell-checking on the performance of content scoring. We systematically vary three sets of influence factors: First, we use either our automatically corrected learner answers as a realistic spell checking scenario or the corrected gold-standard version of the learner answers. We consider the latter an oracle condition to estimate an upper bound of improvement that filters out noise introduced by the spell checker. Second, we use two different feature sets: either the full feature set covering both token and character n-grams or the reduced feature set with only token n-grams. Third, we vary which part of the data is spell-checked. We either correct both the training and the test data or only training or only test data. In the oracle condition, we have only annotations for the test set, so that we use only the test condition here.

Table 6 shows the results. We see that it makes little difference whether we spell-check the data (be it automatically or manually). One possible explanation for the very small difference is that there are many answers without any spelling mistakes at all. Thus, we also comparing the performance for answers with different minimal number of errors. Table 7 shows the breakdown of the results per number of errors. We observe a reduced performance in kappa for answers with more spelling errors, but do not see that repeated in the accuracy, i.e. misclassified answers with more errors have a higher tendency to be completely misclassified.

5.3 Experiment 2 – Simulating Increased Error Frequencies

As we have seen in the above experimental study, there is little difference between the scoring quality on original data vs. spell-checked data. We already ruled out that this might be due to a noisy spell-checker by also evaluating on the annotated gold standard. Another potential reason for our findings is that the amount of errors present in the data is just not large enough to make a difference. To check that, we artificially introduce different amounts of new errors into the learner answers. In this way, we can also simulate corpora with different properties, so that practitioners can check the average amount of spelling errors in their data and can get an estimation of what performance drop to expect.

Generating Spelling Errors In order to generate additional spelling errors, we use two different models:

Random Error Generation introduces errors by either adding, deleting, or substituting a letter or by swapping two letters in randomly selected words. This error generation process is a worst case experiment in the sense that there is no predictable pattern in the produced errors.

Informed Error Generation produces errors according to the distribution of errors in the data. This means we introduce errors only to words that were misspelled in our annotated gold-standard, and we introduce errors by using the misspelled version actually occurring in the data considering the error distribution. In this way, there are chances that – like in real life – some errors will be more frequent than others such that a classifier might be able to learn from them.

We use both models with different configurations of the experimental setup. We vary whether the errors are added to all words (**all**) or only to content words (**cw**). This is because we observed that mainly longer and content words are misspelled. We argue that these words can be more important in content scoring than small function words. Therefore, those realistic errors might do more harm than random errors. In both conditions,

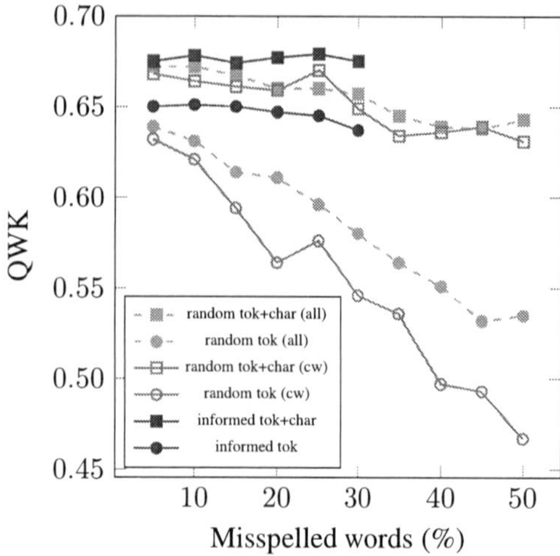

Figure 3: Scoring performance on ASAP with increasing amounts of additional introduced errors.

we make sure that the overall error rate across all tokens matches the desired percentage. Additionally, we use either only token features (**tok**), that will be more sensitive towards spelling errors, or also include the character features (**tok+char**), which we know to be more robust.

Figure 3 shows the performance of the two error generation models in their different variants for different amounts of artificial errors. Note that there was a natural upper bound for the amount of errors which can be introduced using the informed error generator. As expected, we see that content words are more important for scoring than function words as introducing errors to only content words yields a larger performance drop. We see for both generation models that a scoring model using character n-grams is largely robust against spelling mistakes while a model using only information on the token level is not. We also see that a more realistic error generation process is not as detrimental for the scoring performance as random errors. Of course, our error model might be slightly over-optimistic and in real life with such a high number of errors we might see new orthographic variants for individual words that were not covered in our annotations. We therefore believe the realistic curve to be somewhere between the informed and the random model.

6 Related Work

We are not aware of other works studying the impact of spelling errors on content scoring perfor-

mance.

In general, spell checking is often used as a pre-processing step in educational applications, especially those dealing with input written by learners, either non-natives or natives. In some works the influence of spell-checking is explicitly addressed. Pilan et al. (2016) predict the proficiency level of language learners using textbook material as training data and find that spell-checking improves classification performance. Keiper et al. (2016) show that normalizing reading comprehension answers written by language learners is beneficial for POS tagging accuracy.

In some areas however, spelling errors can also be a useful source of information: In the related domain of native language identification, a discipline also dealing with learner texts, Chen et al. (2017) found that spelling errors provide valuable information when determining the native language of an essay's author.

7 Conclusions

We presented a corpus study on spelling errors in the ASAP dataset and provide gold-standard annotations for error detection and correction on large parts of the data.

Next, we examined the influence of spelling errors on content scoring performance. Surprisingly, we found very little influence of spelling mistakes on grading performance for our model and on the ASAP dataset. In our setup, spellchecking seems negligible.

There are several explanations for that: First, we found that we observe a drop in performance if we artificially increase the number of spelling errors. This drop is especially pronounced, if (a) no character n-gram information is used for scoring and (b) if errors follow no specific pattern. If a dataset is expected to contain a higher percentage of spelling errors it will therefore be helpful to correct errors automatically and/or to mitigate the effect of misspelled word by the usage of character n-gram features.

Second, our scoring models relied on shallow features. We assume that scoring models using higher linguistic processing such as dependency triples might suffer more substantially, a question that will be pursued further in future work.

Our gold standard annotations are available under `https://github.com/ltl-ude/asap-spelling` in order to encourage more work on spell-checking in the educational domain.

Acknowledgments

This work is funded by the German Federal Ministry of Education and Research under grant no. FKZ 01PL16075.

References

Lingzhen Chen, Carlo Strapparava, and Vivi Nastase. 2017. Improving native language identification by using spelling errors. In *Proceedings of the 55th Annual Meeting of the Association for Computational Linguistics (Volume 2: Short Papers)*. Association for Computational Linguistics, Vancouver, Canada, pages 542–546. http://aclweb.org/anthology/P17-2086.

Jacob Cohen. 1960. A coefficient of agreement for nominal scales. *Educational and Psychological Measurement* 20(1):37–46.

Jacob Cohen. 1968. Weighted kappa - nominal scale agreement with provision for scaled disagreement or partial credit 70:213–20.

X Conort. 2012. Short answer scoring: Explanation of gxav solution. *ASAP Short Answer Scoring Competition System Description. Retrieved July* 28:2014.

Johannes Daxenberger, Oliver Ferschke, Iryna Gurevych, Torsten Zesch, et al. 2014. Dkpro tc: A java-based framework for supervised learning experiments on textual data. In *ACL (System Demonstrations)*. pages 61–66.

Richard Eckart de Castilho and Iryna Gurevych. 2014. A broad-coverage collection of portable nlp components for building shareable analysis pipelines. In *Proceedings of the Workshop on Open Infrastructures and Analysis Frameworks for HLT (OIAF4HLT) at COLING*. pages 1–11.

Rod Ellis. 1994. *The study of second language acquisition*. Oxford University.

Mark Hall, Eibe Frank, Geoffrey Holmes, Bernhard Pfahringer, Peter Reutemann, and Ian H Witten. 2009. The weka data mining software: an update. *ACM SIGKDD explorations newsletter* 11(1):10–18.

Michael Heilman and Nitin Madnani. 2013. Ets: Domain adaptation and stacking for short answer scoring. In *SemEval@ NAACL-HLT*. pages 275–279.

Derrick Higgins, Chris Brew, Michael Heilman, Ramon Ziai, Lei Chen, Aoife Cahill, Michael Flor, Nitin Madnani, Joel R Tetreault, Daniel Blanchard, Diane Napolitano, Chong Min Lee, and John Blackmore. 2014. Is getting the right answer just about choosing the right words? The role of syntactically-informed features in short answer scoring. *Computation and Language* http://arxiv.org/abs/1403.0801.

Lena Keiper, Andrea Horbach, and Stefan Thater. 2016. Improving pos tagging of german learner language in a reading comprehension scenario. In *LREC*.

Karen Kukich. 1992. Techniques for automatically correcting words in text. *ACM Computing Surveys (CSUR)* 24(4):377–439.

Omer Levy, Torsten Zesch, Ido Dagan, and Iryna Gurevych. 2013. Ukp-biu: Similarity and entailment metrics for student response analysis. In *Second Joint Conference on Lexical and Computational Semantics (* SEM), Volume 2: Proceedings of the Seventh International Workshop on Semantic Evaluation (SemEval 2013)*. volume 2, pages 285–289.

Slav Petrov, Dipanjan Das, and Ryan T. McDonald. 2011. A universal part-of-speech tagset. *CoRR* abs/1104.2086. http://arxiv.org/abs/1104.2086.

Ildiko Pilan, Elena Volodina, and Torsten Zesch. 2016. Predicting proficiency levels in learner writings by transferring a linguistic complexity model from expert-written coursebooks. In *Proceedings of COLING 2016, the 26th International Conference on Computational Linguistics: Technical Papers*. Osaka, Japan, pages 2101 – 2111.

Luis Tandalla. 2012. Scoring short answer essays. *ASAP Short Answer Scoring Competition System Description. Retrieved July* 28:2014.

Seid Muhie Yimam, Iryna Gurevych, Richard Eckart de Castilho, and Chris Biemann. 2013. Webanno: A flexible, web-based and visually supported system for distributed annotations. In *ACL (Conference System Demonstrations)*. pages 1–6.

Jure Zbontar. 2012. Short answer scoring by stacking. *ASAP Short Answer Scoring Competition System Description. Retrieved July* 28:2014.

Analyzing the Impact of Spelling Errors
on POS-Tagging and Chunking in Learner English

Tomoya Mizumoto[1] and **Ryo Nagata**[2] [1]

[1] RIKEN Center for Advanced Intelligence Project
[2] Konan University

`tomoya.mizumoto@riken.jp, nagata-ijcnlp @hyogo-u.ac.jp`

Abstract

Part-of-speech (POS) tagging and chunking have been used in tasks targeting learner English; however, to the best our knowledge, few studies have evaluated their performance and no studies have revealed the causes of POS-tagging/chunking errors in detail. Therefore, we investigate performance and analyze the causes of failure. We focus on spelling errors that occur frequently in learner English. We demonstrate that spelling errors reduced POS-tagging performance by 0.23% owing to spelling errors, and that a spell checker is not necessary for POS-tagging/chunking of learner English.

1 Introduction

Part-of-speech (POS) tagging and chunking have been essential components of Natural Language Processing (NLP) techniques that target learner English, such as grammatical error correction and automated essay scoring. In addition, they are frequently used to extract linguistic features relevant to the given task. For example, in the CoNLL-2014 Shared Task (Ng et al., 2014), 10 of the 12 teams used one or both POS-tagging and chunking to extract features for grammatical error correction.

They have also been used for linguistic analysis of learner English, particularly in corpus-based studies. Aarts and Granger (1998) explored characteristic POS patterns in learner English. Nagata and Whittaker (2013) demonstrated that POS sequences obtained by POS-tagging can be used to distinguish between mother tongue interferences effectively.

The heavy dependence on POS-tagging and chunking suggests that failures could degrade the performance of NLP systems and linguistic analyses (Han et al., 2006; Sukkarieh and Blackmore, 2009). For example, failure to recognize noun phrases in a sentence could lead to failure in correcting related errors in article use and noun number. More importantly, such failures make it more difficult to simply count the number of POSs and chunks, thereby causing inaccurate estimates of their distributions. Note that such estimates are often employed in linguistic analysis, including the above-mentioned studies.

Despite its importance in related tasks, we also note that few studies have focused on performance evaluations of POS-tagging and chunking. Only a few studies, including Nagata et al. (2011), Berzak et al. (2016) and Sakaguchi et al. (2012), have reported the performance of POS taggers in learner English and found a performance gap between native and learner English. However, none of those studies described the root causes of POS-tagging and chunking errors in detail. Detailed investigations would certainly improve performance, which in turn, would improve related tasks. Furthermore, to the best of our knowledge, no study has reported chunking performance when applied to learner English. [1]

Unknown words are a major cause of POS-tagging and chunking failures (Manning, 2011). In learner English, spelling errors, which occur frequently, are a major source of unknown words.

Spell checkers (e.g., Aspell) are used to correct spelling errors prior to POS-tagging and chunking. However, their effectiveness remains unclear.

Thus, we evaluate the extent to which spelling errors in learner English affect the POS tag-

---

[1] It appears that parsing doubles as chunking; however, chunking only considers a minimal phrase (non-recursive structures).

Proceedings of the 4th Workshop on Natural Language Processing Techniques for Educational Applications, pages 54–58,
Taipei, Taiwan, December 1, 2017 ©2017 AFNLP

ging and chunking performance. More precisely, we analyze the performance analysis of POS-tagging/chunking to determine (1) the extent to which performance is reduced due to spelling errors, (2) what types of spelling errors impact the performance, and (3) the effect of correcting spelling errors using a spell checker. Our analysis demonstrates that employing a spell checker is not required preliminary step of POS-tagging and chunking for NLP analysis of learner English.

2 Performance Analysis of Spelling Errors

Here, we explain how we analyzed POS tagging/chunking performance relative to spelling errors.

Extent of performance degradation due to spelling errors Spelling errors occur frequently in learner English. For example, the learner corpus used in (Flor et al., 2013) includes 3.4% spelling errors. Thus assuming that POS-tagging and chunking fails for all unknown words, performance would be reduced by 3.4% owing spelling errors. Realistically, performance does not drop a full 3.4% because POS-taggers and chunkers can infer POS/chunk from surrounding words. However, it is not clear how POS-tagging/chunking can correctly predict them. In contrast, if it is possible to estimate POSs/chunks of misspelled words from surrounding words, this has the potential to fail due to spelling errors. To investigate the extent to which performance is reduced due to spelling errors, we compared the results of POS-tagging and chunking on learner English without correcting spelling errors to results obtained by POS-tagging and chunking on learner English in which spelling errors were first corrected. In addition, we measured the effect of misspelled words had on them or their surrounding words by counting the number of correctly identified POSs/chunks.

Types of spelling errors There are various types of spelling errors in learner English (Sakaguchi et al., 2012). The most common type of spelling error is a typographical error (e.g., *studing/studying). In learner English, other types of errors include homophones (e.g., *see/sea), confusion (e.g., *form/from), splits (e.g., *home town/hometown), merges (e.g., *airconditioner/air conditioner), inflections (e.g., *program/programming) and derivations (e.g.,

*smell/smelly).[2] Some spelling errors, such as typographical and merge errors, result in unknown words, whereas others, such as homophones and split errors, are known words. For unknown words, it is possible to predict POSs/chunks from surrounding words, whereas for known words (e.g., homophone errors), POS-tagging/chunking fails. We use specific examples to investigate what types of spelling errors impact the performance of POS-tagging.

Some spelling errors have effective information that helps determine POSs. For example, for the above typographical error (i.e., *studing/studying), it may be possible to predict the corresponding POS as a "gerund or present participle verb" based on the suffix "ing." We also consider the effectiveness of prefix and suffix (i.e., affix) information in determining the corresponding POS for misspelled words. For this investigation, we compared POS-tagging systems both with and without affix information.

Effects of a spell checker Some previous studies into grammatical error correction investigated using a spell checker in a preprocessing step to reduce the negative impact of spelling errors. However, as noted above, little is known about the performance of POS-tagging and chunking for misspelled words and their surrounding words. Therefore, the effectiveness of a spell checker in a preprocessing step on POS-tagging and chunking for learner English remains unclear. Spell checkers can correct some errors, particularly unknown word errors; thus, POS-tagging and chunking have the potential to predict correct tags. We therefore examined the effect of a spell checker has on POS-tagging and chunking performance by comparing results obtained with and without the use of a spell checker.

3 Experimental Setup

To evaluate the performance of POS-tagging and chunking, we used the Konan-JIEM (KJ) corpus (Nagata et al., 2011), which consists of 3,260 sentences and 30,517 tokens. Note that the essays in the KJ corpus were written by Japanese university students. The number of spelling errors targeted in this paper was 654 (i.e., 2.1% of all words).

We used a proprietary dataset comprising English teaching materials for reading comprehen-

---

[2]Note that we do not address split and merge errors.

#TP	#FP	#FN	Precision	Recall	F-score
409	197	120	67.49	77.32	72.07

Table 1: Performance of spelling error correction

sion for Japanese students. We annotated this dataset with POS tags and chunks to train a model for POS-tagging and chunking. This corpus consists of 16,375 sentences and 213,017 tokens, and does not contain grammatical errors. We also used sections 0-18 of the Penn TreeBank only to train the model for POS-tagging.

We formulated the POS-tagging and chunking as a sequence labeling problem. We used a conditional random field (CRF) (Lafferty et al., 2001) for sequence labeling and CRF++[3] with default parameters as a CRF tool. The features used for POS-tagging were based on the widely used features employed in Ratnaparkhi (1996). These features consist of surface, original form, presence of specific characters (e.g., numbers, uppercase, and symbols), and prefix and suffix (i.e., affix) information. In addition to (Ratnaparkhi, 1996), we used the original forms of words as features. For the chunking task, we also employed generally used features in this case from Sha and Pereira (2003). These features were based on surface, the original form of the words and POSs. These features are used in which tools are commonly used for grammatical error correction tasks.

We also developed a spell checker for our experiments. We constructed the spell checker based on a noisy channel model to capture the influence of spelling errors originating via the mother tongue. Table 1 summarizes the spelling correction performance of the spell checker on the KJ corpus. As can be seen, better performance results is demonstrated compared to Sakaguchi et al. (2012). In most previous research into grammatical error correction, a spell checker is used in a pipeline. Therefore, we used this pipeline method and treated spelling correction and POS-tagging and chunking as cascading problems.

For our evaluation metrics, we used accuracy (number of correct tokens / number of tokens in the corpus). In addition, we counted the number of correct tokens identified despite spelling errors, as well as their preceding and succeeding tokens, to observe the effect of spelling errors had on their surrounding words.

[3]https://taku910.github.io/crfpp/

Method	Accuracy
Baseline	93.97 (92.71)
Base+Aff	95.31 (93.93)
Base+Checker	94.21 (93.13)
Base+Aff+Checker	95.37 (94.05)
Base+Aff+Gold	**95.54 (94.16)**

Table 2: Results of POS-tagging. Accuracies of POS-tagging trained on Penn TreeBank are shown in parentheses.

Method	# of s_i correct	# of s_{i-1} correct	# of s_{i+1} correct
Baseline	344	540	590
Base+Aff	465	542	598
Base+Aff+Gold	528	547	596

Table 3: Results of POS tagging for misspelled words and their surrounding words. s_i indicates a misspelled word.

4 POS-tagging Experiments

We conducted POS-tagging experiments to investigate the question introduced in Section 2. We prepared the following five methods:

1. A POS-tagging system trained with surface, original form, and presence of particular character features (**Baseline**)

2. A system with prefix and suffix (affix) features added to the *Baseline* (**Base+Aff**)

3. The *Baseline* POS-tagging system with a spell checker (**Base+Checker**)

4. The *Base+Aff* POS-tagging system with a spell checker (**Base+Aff+Checker**)

5. The *Base+Aff* POS-tagging system without a spell checker, i.e., errors were corrected manually (**Base+Aff+Gold**)

Table 2 summarizes the experimental results for POS-tagging. The results show the same tendency for POS-tagging trained on in-house data and POS-tagging trained on Penn TreeBank, i.e., Base+Aff+Gold > Base+Aff+Checker > Base+Aff > Base+Checker > Baseline. Therefore, to simplifying analysis, we used results obtained with the in-house data. First, we compared *Base+Aff* to *Base+Aff+Gold* to determine the influence of spelling errors. *Base+Aff+Gold* achieved a 0.23% improvement over *Base+Aff*. From this, we conclude that the POS-tagging performance dropped 0.23% due to spelling errors.

This also indicates that an ideal spell checker does have a positive impact on POS-tagging.

We also observed that *Base+Aff* demonstrated 1.3% higher accuracy compared to *Baseline*. Similarly, *Base+Aff* showed higher accuracy than that of *Base+Checker*. These results indicate that affix information is important to assigning corresponding POSs in learner English. Furthermore, there was only a difference of only 0.06% between *Base+Aff* and *Base+Aff+Checker*, thereby demonstrating that a spell checker is not necessary and that it is sufficient to assign POSs using affix information.

Table 3 shows the number of correct POSs identified for misspelled and surrounding words. As can be seen by comparing the *Baseline* to *Base+Aff+Gold*, the number of correct POSs for misspelled words increased. In contrast, for the number of correct POSs identified for surrounding words, there was nearly no difference, implying that spelling errors do not influence the accuracy of estimating the POSs of their surrounding words.

Types of spelling errors that affect performance
We first compared *Baseline* to *Base+Aff* to observe spelling errors that can be corrected with affix information. The numbers of correct POSs for *Baseline* and *Base+Aff* were 344 and 465, respectively. Therefore, by using affix information, we could identify the correct POS for approximately 120 misspelled words. Two examples in which the *Baseline* failed in POS-tagging but *Base+Aff* succeeded are shown in the following.

> (1) a. Winter is decolat<u>ed</u>/***Verb, past*** ...
>   b. Accod<u>ing</u>/***Verb, gerund*** to ...

Here, the POS-tagger was able to assign correct POSs to misspelled words using affix information. Both *decolated* (*decorated) and *Accoding* (*According) were inferred via the *ed* and *ing* suffixes, respectively.

Next, we analyzed the output of *Base+Aff* and *Base+Aff+Gold* to identify spelling errors that make it difficult to predict POS-tags. The number of POSs that *Base+Aff* failed to identify in POS-tagging but *Base+Aff+Gold* identified successfully was 105. We divided these 105 errors into five types according to the cause of the failure. The most frequent cause (54 instances) was unknown words from spelling errors (e.g., evey). The remaining causes of failure were as follows: 20 errors in which a POS was predicted based on

affix features (e.g., whiting), 17 errors due to different words (e.g., thought→though), 10 errors in which the POS was predicted based on the presence of uppercase characters (e.g., Exsample), and three errors caused by romanized Japanese words.

Effect of spelling correction by spell checker
We analyzed spelling errors where POS-tagging failed in the system with affix information but the system with the spell checker succeeded. The number of spelling errors that were correctly assigned to POSs with the spell checker was 74, whereas the number of spelling errors incorrectly assigned a POS was 49. The system with the spell checker correctly assigned a POS to the following:

> (2) a. pepole/***Noun, singular*** → people/***Noun, plural***
>   b. tow/***Noun, singular*** apples→ two/***Numeral*** apples

These examples show cases in which spelling errors were corrected by the spell checker. As mentioned previously, these spelling errors are examples of words in which POS-tagging failed due to unknown words. Examples in which POS-tagging with the spell checker failed involved the spell checker changing misspelled words to different but incorrect words (e.g., *tero* → *to* (correct is *terrorist*), *tittle* → *little* (correct is *title*)).

5   Chunking Experiments

As with the POS-tagging experiments, we performed chunking experiments on learner English. As described in Section 1, we examined the performance of chunking in learner English for the first time. We compared the following three systems: (1) a system using the features presented in Section 3 (**Baseline**), (2) a baseline chunking

---

Method	Accuracy
Baseline	94.38
Base+Checker	94.41
Base+Gold	**94.58**

Table 4: Chunking results

Method	# of s_i correct	# of s_{i-1} correct	# of s_{i+1} correct
Baseline	532	504	565
Base+Gold	566	519	570

Table 5: Results of chunking involving misspelled words, as well as corresponding preceding and succeeding words.

system with spell checking (**Base+Checker**), and (3) a baseline chunking system with no spelling errors, i.e., spelling errors were corrected manually (**Base+Gold**). We used POSs that were automatically assigned by the POS-tagger[4] to train our chunking model.

The experimental results on chunking are summarized in Table 4. As can be seen by comparing *Baseline* to *Base+Checker*, there was only a 0.03% difference, which has no statistical significance; thus, the spell checker had nearly no practical effect. Comparing *Baseline* to *Base+Gold*, there was a difference of 0.2% which is statistically significant even though it is only a small difference. Thus, we conclude here that an ideal spell checker has a positive effect on chunking. However, since chunking uses POSs identified by the POS-tagger as its features, it was assumed that POS-tagging errors would directly affect chunking. Table 5 shows the number of correctly identified chunks for misspelled and surrounding words. As with POS-tagging, the number of correctly identified chunks for misspelled words increased, whereas there was nearly no difference in the number of correctly identified chunks for surrounding words.

6 Conclusions

In this paper, we have investigated the performance of POS-tagging and chunking in learner English. The primary cause of failures in POS-tagging and chunking is well known to be unknown words; thus, we focused our investigation on spelling errors, which are the primary sources of unknown words. Furthermore, we have demonstrated the performance of chunking in learner English for, to the best of our knowledge, the first time. From our experiments, we conclude that POS-tagging performance dropped 0.23% due to spelling errors. Furthermore a spell checker is not necessary for POS-tagging, and it is sufficient to assign POS-tags using affix information.

References

Jan Aarts and Sylviane Granger. 1998. Tag sequences in learner corpora: a key to interlanguage grammar and discourse. In Sylviane Granger, editor, *Learner English on Computer*, pages 132–141. Addison Wesley Longman: London and New York.

Yevgeni Berzak, Jessica Kenney, Carolyn Spadine, Jing Xian Wang, Lucia Lam, Keiko Sophie Mori, Sebastian Garza, and Boris Katz. 2016. Universal Dependencies for Learner English. In *Proceedings of ACL*, pages 737–746.

Michael Flor, Yoko Futagi, Melissa Lopez, and Matthew Mulholland. 2013. Patterns of misspellings in L2 and L1 English: a view from the ETS Spelling Corpus. In *the Second Learner Corpus Research Conference*.

Na-Rae Han, Martin Chodorow, and Claudia Leacock. 2006. Detecting Errors in English Article Usage by Non-Native Speakers. *Natural Language Engineering*, 12(2):115–129.

John D. Lafferty, Andrew McCallum, and Fernando C. N. Pereira. 2001. Conditional Random Fields: Probabilistic Models for Segmenting and Labeling Sequence Data. In *Proceedings of ICML*, pages 282–289.

Christopher Manning. 2011. Part-of-Speech Tagging from 97% to 100%: Is It Time for Some Linguistics? In *Proceedings of CICLing*, pages 171–189.

Ryo Nagata and Edward Whittaker. 2013. Reconstructing an Indo-European Family Tree from Non-native English Texts. In *Proceedings of ACL*, pages 1137–1147.

Ryo Nagata, Edward Whittaker, and Vera Sheinman. 2011. Creating a Manually Error-tagged and shallow-parsed corpus. In *Proceedings of ACL-HLT*, pages 1210–1219.

Hwee Tou Ng, Siew Mei Wu, Ted Briscoe, Christian Hadiwinoto, Raymond Hendy Susanto, and Christopher Bryant. 2014. The CoNLL-2014 Shared Task on Grammatical Error Correction. In *Proceedings of CoNLL Shared Task*, pages 1–14.

Adwait Ratnaparkhi. 1996. A Maximum Entropy Model for Part-Of-Speech Tagging. In *Proceedings of EMNLP*, pages 133–142.

Keisuke Sakaguchi, Tomoya Mizumoto, Mamoru Komachi, and Yuji Matsumoto. 2012. Joint English Spelling Error Correction and POS Tagging for Language Learners Writing. In *Proceedings of COLING*, pages 2357–2374.

Fei Sha and Fernando Pereira. 2003. Shallow Parsing with Conditional Random Fields. In *Proceedings of HLT-NAACL*, pages 134–141.

Jana Z. Sukkarieh and John Blackmore. 2009. c-rater: Automatic Content Scoring for Short Constructed Responses. In *Proceedings of FLAIRS*, pages 290–295.

---

[4]The POS-tagger was trained with all features.

Complex Word Identification:
Challenges in Data Annotation and System Performance

Marcos Zampieri[1], Shervin Malmasi[2], Gustavo Paetzold[3], Lucia Specia[3]
[1]University of Wolverhampton, United Kingdom
[2]Harvard Medical School, United States
[3]University of Sheffield, United Kingdom
`m.zampieri@wlv.ac.uk, smalmasi@bwh.harvard.edu`
`g.h.paetzold@sheffield.ac.uk, l.specia@sheffield.ac.uk`

Abstract

This paper revisits the problem of complex word identification (CWI) following up the SemEval CWI shared task. We use ensemble classifiers to investigate how well computational methods can discriminate between complex and non-complex words. Furthermore, we analyze the classification performance to understand what makes lexical complexity challenging. Our findings show that most systems performed poorly on the SemEval CWI dataset, and one of the reasons for that is the way in which human annotation was performed.

1 Introduction

Lexical complexity plays a crucial role in reading comprehension. Several NLP systems have been developed to simplify texts to second language learners (Petersen and Ostendorf, 2007) and to native speakers with low literacy levels (Specia, 2010) and reading disabilities (Rello et al., 2013). Identifying which words are likely to be considered complex by a given target population is an important task in many text simplification pipelines called complex word identification (CWI). CWI has been addressed as a stand-alone task (Shardlow, 2013) and as part of studies in lexical and text simplification (Paetzold, 2016).

The recent SemEval 2016 Task 11 on Complex Word Identification – henceforth SemEval CWI – addressed this challenge by providing participants with a manually annotated dataset for this purpose (Paetzold and Specia, 2016a). In the SemEval CWI dataset, words in context were tagged as complex or non-complex, that is, difficult to be understood by non-native English speakers, or not. Participating teams used this dataset to train classi-

fiers to predict lexical complexity assigning a label 0 to non-complex words and 1 to complex ones. Below is an example instance from their dataset:

(1) A **frenulum** is a small fold of tissue that secures or **restricts** the **motion** of a mobile organ in the body.

The words in bold — *frenulum, restricts, motion* — have been assigned by at least one of the annotators as complex and thus they were labeled as such in the training set. All words that have not been assigned by at least one annotator as complex have been labeled as non-complex.

In this paper we evaluate the dataset annotation and the performance of systems participating in the SemEval CWI task. We first estimate the theoretical upper bound performance of the task given the output of the SemEval systems. Secondly, we investigate whether human annotation correlates to the systems' performance by carefully analyzing the samples of multiple annotators. Although in the shared task complexity was modeled as a binary classification task, we pose that lexical complexity should actually be seen in a continuum spectrum. Intuitively, words that are labeled as complex more often should be easier to be predicted by CWI systems. This hypothesis is investigated in Section 3.3. To the best of our knowledge, no evaluation of this kind has been carried out for CWI. The most similar analyses to ours have been carried out by Malmasi et al. (2015) for native language identification and by Goutte et al. (2016) for language variety identification.

2 Methods and Experiments

In this section we present the data, the methods, and an overview of the experiments we propose in this paper. The goal of the experiments is to evaluate CWI performance with respect to computational methods and the manual annotation of the

Proceedings of the 4th Workshop on Natural Language Processing Techniques for Educational Applications, pages 59–63,
Taipei, Taiwan, December 1, 2017 ©2017 AFNLP

Team	Approach	System Paper
SV000gg	System voting with threshold and machine learning-based classifiers trained on morphological, lexical, and semantic features	(Paetzold and Specia, 2016b)
TALN	Random forests of lexical, morphological, semantic & syntactic features	(Ronzano et al., 2016)
UWB	Maximum Entropy classifiers trained over word occurrence counts on Wikipedia documents	(Konkol, 2016)
PLUJAGH	Threshold-based methods trained on Simple Wikipedia	(Wróbel, 2016)
JUNLP	Random Forest and Naive Bayes classifiers trained over semantic, lexicon-based, morphological and syntactic features	(Mukherjee et al., 2016)
HMC	Decision trees trained over lexical, semantic, syntactic and psycholinguistic features	(Quijada and Medero, 2016)
MACSAAR	Random Forest and SVM classifiers trained over Zipfian features	(Zampieri et al., 2016)
Pomona	Threshold-based bagged classifiers with bootstrap re-sampling trained over word frequencies	(Kauchak, 2016)
Melbourne	Weighted Random Forests trained on lexical/semantic features	(Brooke et al., 2016)
IIIT	Nearest Centroid classifiers trained over semantic and morphological features	(Palakurthi and Mamidi, 2016)

Table 1: SemEval CWI - Systems and approaches

dataset. For this purpose we build a plurality ensemble and an oracle classifier and subsequently analyze systems output using the manual annotation provided by the SemEval CWI organizers.

2.1 Data

The dataset compiled for the shared task contains a training set composed of 2,237 instances and a test set of 88,221 instances. The data was collected through on-line questionnaires in which 400 non-native English speakers were presented with several sentences and asked to select which words they did not understand the meaning of. Annotators were students and staff of various universities. The training set is composed by the judgments of 20 distinct annotators over a set of 200 sentences, while the test set is composed by the judgments made over 9,000 sentences by only one annotator.

The 9,200 sentences were evenly distributed across the 400 annotators. In the training set, a word is considered to be complex if at least one of the 20 annotators judged them so, thus reproducing a scenario that captures one of the biggest challenges in lexical simplification: predicting the vocabulary limitations of individuals based on the overall limitations of a group. This dataset is one of the few datasets available for CWI, another example is the one by Yimam et al. (2017).

2.2 Systems

The SemEval CWI shared task provided an opportunity to compare the performance of CWI approaches using a common dataset. It was the first and only challenge organized on the topic thus far.

The task was very popular, having attracted 21 teams and 42 participating systems. In Table 1 we present the 10 highest performing approaches proposed by participants of the SemEval CWI task.

2.3 Approaches

We build ensemble classifiers taking the output of systems that participated in the SemEval CWI task as input. This approach is equivalent to training multiple classifiers and combining them using ensembles. Our first goal is to build high-performance classifiers using plurality voting. Our second goal is to estimate the theoretical upper bound performance given the output of the systems that participated in the SemEval CWI competition using the oracle classifier. Following Malmasi et al. (2015) and Goutte et al. (2016) we use two approaches:

Plurality Voting: This approach selects the label with the highest number of votes, regardless of the percentage of votes it received (Polikar, 2006).

Oracle: It assigns the correct label for an instance if at least one of the classifiers produces the correct label for the given data point. It serves to quantify the theoretical upper limit performance on a given dataset (Kuncheva et al., 2001).

3 Results

3.1 Plurality Voting

We first test the plurality voting ensemble using the output of all 46 entries (42 runs plus 4 baselines) submitted to the CWI task. We also built a plurality ensemble system using only the output of the top 10 systems. Our assumption was that including systems that did not perform well in the task degrades the voting performance by introducing too much noise in the predictions.

Plurality voting results for class 1 are presented in Table 2 in terms of precision, recall, and F1 score. For comparison we also report a threshold-based baseline on word frequencies from Wikipedia (Paetzold and Specia, 2016a) and the performance of the best system in terms of f-score for class 1. The number of instances in each class is presented in the column 'Samples'.

System	Class	P	R	F1	Samples
All	0	0.98	0.83	0.90	84,090
All	1	0.17	0.71	0.27	4,131
Top 10	0	0.98	0.88	0.93	84,090
Top 10	1	0.21	0.66	0.32	4,131
Baseline	1	0.08	0.90	0.15	4,131
Best	1	0.29	0.45	0.35	4,131

Table 2: Results for plurality voting

The results obtained show that the plurality voting system performs significantly better on class 0 (non-complex words) achieving 0.90 F1 score than on class 1 (complex words) achieving 0.27 F1 score. The majority of instances in the dataset are non-complex words and this explains the bias. For class 1, the F1 score obtained by the ensemble featuring the top 10 systems outperforms the baseline but it is outperformed by the best system by 3 percentage points.

3.2 Optimal Ensemble and Oracle

We showed the performance of plurality voting ensembles built with the output of all systems and with the output of the top-10 ranked systems. The setup using the output of the top-10 systems yielded very good performance, but still below the best system in the competition. In this section we investigate how many systems should be included in the ensemble to obtain the best possible performance. In Figure 1 we show the F1-score, precision, and recall results for class 1 obtained by plurality voting using ensemble configurations ranging from 3 to 46 systems.

To investigate the optimal ensemble configuration we performed a greedy backward search over the systems, iteratively removing the worst systems in a stepwise manner without a stopping criterion. The best performance for complex words was obtained using with the predictions of the top-

3 systems achieving 0.35 F1-score. This is the best performing and smallest ensemble configuration confirming that the SemEval CWI is a very challenging task which led the vast majority of systems to perform so poorly that the plurality voting ensemble did not benefit from their predictions.

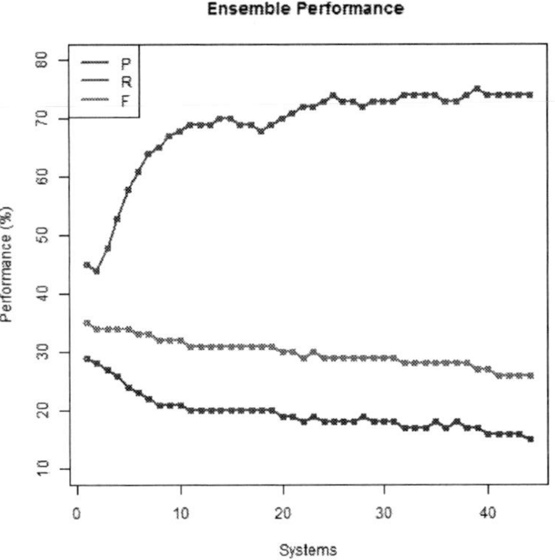

Figure 1: Plurality voting using n best systems

Finally, in Table 3 we present the results obtained by the oracle classifier using the top-3 systems, which yielded the best results in the plurality voting ensemble. The oracle performs very well when predicting non-complex words achieving 0.98 F1-score. The performance for complex words was substantially higher than the one obtained using the configurations of the plurality voting ensemble, reaching 0.60 F1-score and outperforming both the baseline and the best system. This is the theoretical upper bound of the task given the output of the systems that used this dataset.

System	Class	P	R	F1	Samples
Oracle	0	0.98	0.98	0.98	84,090
Oracle	1	0.59	0.61	0.60	4,131
Baseline	1	0.08	0.90	0.15	4,131
Best	1	0.29	0.45	0.35	4,131

Table 3: Results for oracle classifier (top-3)

3.3 Lexical Complexity

In this section we investigate features of the dataset and annotation that influence the output of the classifiers using the training set and the results of the 10 best performing systems. We start by looking at an histogram of annotations of all complex words in the training data (Figure 2).

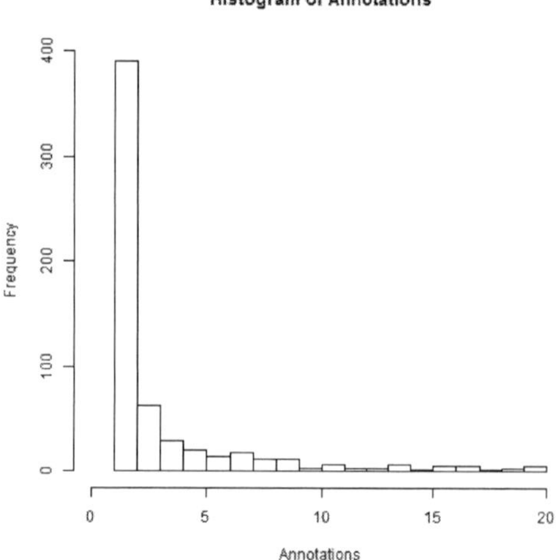

Figure 2: Histogram of annotations.

Among the 2,237 words in the training set, 706 were labeled as complex. The histogram shows the distribution of the annotation that ranged from 393 words labeled by 1 annotator as complex and only 5 words labeled by all 20 annotators as such.

Inspired by readability metrics (Kincaid et al., 1975), we looked at the average word length (AWL) of the words in the training set under the assumption that longer words tend to be more often perceived as complex. We divide the dataset in intervals according to the number of annotators that assigned each word as complex: 10-20, 1-9, and none. Results are presented in Table 4.

Class	Annotators	Words	AWL
1	10-20	42	7.07
1	1-9	664	6.71
1	1-20	706	6.74
0	0	1,531	5.94

Table 4: Word length and complexity

We observed that words that were assigned as complex are on average longer than non-complex ones. Complex words in the dataset are on average 6.74 characters long whereas non-complex words are on average 5.94 characters long.

Finally, we investigate the interplay between annotation and system performance by analyzing the 38 words in the training data which were labeled as complex by at least half of the annotators. We 1) check the overlap of these words in the training and test sets; 2) verify how many overlap-

ping words received the same label in the training and test sets; 3) compute the number of times humans annotated a given word as complex (0-20) and the number of top-10 systems that labeled the word as complex (0-10). We present the scores for the words that met these criteria in Table 5. For comparison we also present five randomly selected words labeled as complex by only one annotator which received the same label in the train and test sets.

Word	Humans	Systems
gharial	20	10
khachkar	17	10
anoxic	14	10
ubiquitous	12	8
rebuffed	11	10
took	1	0
better	1	0
however	1	0
designation	1	4
islands	1	0

Table 5: Annotation vs. prediction.

The CWI dataset replicates a scenario in which the vocabulary limitations of individuals is assessed based on the overall limitations of a group, as a result 50% of the most complex words did not receive the same label in the training and test sets. Nevertheless, the results of this pilot analysis seem to confirm our hypothesis that words that were tagged more often as complex in the training set tend to be easier for CWI system to identify.

4 Conclusion and Future Work

This paper complements the findings from the SemEval CWI shared task report (Paetzold and Specia, 2016a) by presenting an evaluation of CWI system outputs and of the dataset used in the shared task. We were able to: 1) estimate the potential upper limit of the task considering the output of the participating systems (0.60 F1 score for complex words); 2) provide empirical evidence of the relation between word length and lexical complexity for this dataset; and 3) confirm that the performance of CWI systems in this shared task is related to non-native speakers' annotation.

Our findings serve as a starting point for a potential re-run of the SemEval CWI task and for other studies using the 2016 dataset. In future work we would like to investigate other factors that influence lexical complexity such as word frequency and grammatical categories.

Acknowledgements

This contribution was partially supported by the European Commission project SIMPATICO (H2020-EURO-6-2015, grant number 692819). We would like to thank the anonymous reviewers for their feedback.

References

Julian Brooke, Alexandra Uitdenbogerd, and Timothy Baldwin. 2016. Melbourne at semeval 2016 task 11: Classifying type-level word complexity using random forests with corpus and word list features. In *Proceedings of the 10th International Workshop on Semantic Evaluation (SemEval-2016)*, pages 975–981, San Diego, California. Association for Computational Linguistics.

Cyril Goutte, Serge Léger, Shervin Malmasi, and Marcos Zampieri. 2016. Discriminating Similar Languages: Evaluations and Explorations. In *Proceedings of LREC*.

David Kauchak. 2016. Pomona at semeval-2016 task 11: Predicting word complexity based on corpus frequency. In *Proceedings of the 10th SemEval*, pages 1047–1051.

J Peter Kincaid, Robert P Fishburne Jr, Richard L Rogers, and Brad S Chissom. 1975. Derivation of New Readability Formulas (Automated Readability Index, Fog Count and Flesch Reading Ease Formula) for Navy Enlisted Personnel. Technical report, Naval Technical Training Command Millington TN Research Branch.

Michal Konkol. 2016. Uwb at semeval-2016 task 11: Exploring features for complex word identification. In *Proceedings of the 10th SemEval*, pages 1038–1041.

Ludmila I Kuncheva, James C Bezdek, and Robert PW Duin. 2001. Decision Templates for Multiple Classifier Fusion: An Experimental Comparison. *Pattern Recognition*, 34(2):299–314.

Shervin Malmasi, Joel Tetreault, and Mark Dras. 2015. Oracle and Human Baselines for Native Language Identification. In *Proceedings of the BEA workshop*.

Niloy Mukherjee, Braja Gopal Patra, Dipankar Das, and Sivaji Bandyopadhyay. 2016. Ju_nlp at semeval-2016 task 11: Identifying complex words in a sentence. In *Proceedings of the 10th SemEval*, pages 986–990.

Gustavo Henrique Paetzold. 2016. *Lexical Simplification for Non-Native English Speakers*. Ph.D. thesis, University of Sheffield.

Gustavo Henrique Paetzold and Lucia Specia. 2016a. SemEval 2016 Task 11: Complex Word Identification. In *Proceedings of SemEval*.

Gustavo Henrique Paetzold and Lucia Specia. 2016b. SV000gg at SemEval-2016 Task 11: Heavy Gauge Complex Word Identification with System Voting. In *Proceedings of the 10th SemEval*, pages 969–974.

Ashish Palakurthi and Radhika Mamidi. 2016. Iiit at semeval-2016 task 11: Complex word identification using nearest centroid classification. In *Proceedings of the 10th SemEval*, pages 1017–1021.

Sarah E Petersen and Mari Ostendorf. 2007. Text Simplification for Language Learners: A Corpus Analysis. In *Proceedings of SLaTE*.

Robi Polikar. 2006. Ensemble Based Systems in Decision Making. *Circuits and systems magazine, IEEE*, 6(3):21–45.

Maury Quijada and Julie Medero. 2016. Hmc at semeval-2016 task 11: Identifying complex words using depth-limited decision trees. In *Proceedings of the 10th SemEval*, pages 1034–1037.

Luz Rello, Ricardo Baeza-Yates, Stefan Bott, and Horacio Saggion. 2013. Simplify or Help?: Text Simplification Strategies for People with Dyslexia. In *Proceedings of W4A*.

Francesco Ronzano, Ahmed Abura'ed, Luis Espinosa Anke, and Horacio Saggion. 2016. Taln at semeval-2016 task 11: Modelling complex words by contextual, lexical and semantic features. In *Proceedings of the 10th SemEval*, pages 1011–1016.

Matthew Shardlow. 2013. A Comparison of Techniques to Automatically Identify Complex Words. In *Proceedings of the ACL Student Research Workshop*.

Lucia Specia. 2010. Translating from Complex to Simplified Sentences. *Computational Processing of the Portuguese Language*, pages 30–39.

Krzysztof Wróbel. 2016. Plujagh at semeval-2016 task 11: Simple system for complex word identification. In *Proceedings of the 10th SemEval*, pages 953–957.

Seid Muhie Yimam, Sanja Štajner, Martin Riedl, and Chris Biemann. 2017. Multilingual and Cross-Lingual Complex Word Identification. In *Proceedings of RANLP*.

Marcos Zampieri, Liling Tan, and Josef van Genabith. 2016. Macsaar at semeval-2016 task 11: Zipfian and character features for complexword identification. In *Proceedings of the 10th SemEval*, pages 1001–1005.

Suggesting Sentences for ESL using Kernel Embeddings

Kent Shioda and **Mamoru Komachi** and **Rue Ikeya** and **Daichi Mochihashi**

{shioda-kent@ed., komachi@}tmu.ac.jp
ikeya@nii.ac.jp, daichi@ism.ac.jp

Abstract

Sentence retrieval is an important NLP application for English as a Second Language (ESL) learners. ESL learners are familiar with web search engines, but generic web search results may not be adequate for composing documents in a specific domain. However, if we build our own search system specialized to a domain, it may be subject to the data sparseness problem. Recently proposed word2vec partially addresses the data sparseness problem, but fails to extract sentences relevant to queries owing to the modeling of the latent intent of the query. Thus, we propose a method of retrieving example sentences using kernel embeddings and N-gram windows. This method implicitly models latent intent of query and sentences, and alleviates the problem of noisy alignment. Our results show that our method achieved higher precision in sentence retrieval for ESL in the domain of a university press release corpus, as compared to a previous unsupervised method used for a semantic textual similarity task.

1 Introduction

Many English writing assistant tools are currently being studied and developed. However, even for advanced ESL learners, it is difficult to write sentences conforming to the styles and expressions in a specific domain. Therefore, it is beneficial for non-native speakers to search for sentences using keywords that the writer aims to use.

However, existing sentence retrieval systems fail to capture the latent intent of query, owing to the modeling of sentences. We address this problem by using a kernel embeddings framework. Kernel embeddings makes it possible to add expression to the query in sentence retrieval by using latent probability distribution. In addition, our method of taking N-gram windows boosts the precision of sentence retrieval by considering words that are highly related to the query.

The main contributions of this study are as follows:

- We propose a novel sentence similarity metric based on kernel embeddings and N-gram windows.

- We build a corpus of university press releases and annotated example sentences for ESL, given a query of two words.

- We show that our proposed method outperforms unsupervised baselines on our dataset.

2 Proposed Method

To address the problem of query intent, we propose a sentence retrieval method that considers the latent distribution of a sentence using kernel embeddings. Our proposed method calculates the similarity between the keywords and the target sentences in a high dimensional space defined by kernels using the latent distribution of the query. In addition, our system only requires several keywords as an input, and finds a relevant sentence based on N-grams in the sentence.

In the following subsections, we first describe how we adopt kernel embeddings for sentence retrieval, and then explain how to incorporate N-gram windows to improve the precision of sentence retrieval.

2.1 Kernel Embeddings

Yoshikawa et al. (2015) proposed a method to calculate the similarity between instances across different domains by embedding all the features of

Proceedings of the 4th Workshop on Natural Language Processing Techniques for Educational Applications, pages 64–68,
Taipei, Taiwan, December 1, 2017 ©2017 AFNLP

different domains into a shared latent space. Their approach, which calculates the similarity between instances in shared latent space, employed the kernel embeddings framework of Smola et al. (2007). The kernel embeddings of distributions are used to embed any probability distribution $\mathbb{P}$ on space $\mathcal{X}$ into a reproducing kernel Hilbert space (RKHS) $\mathcal{H}_k$ specified by kernel k, where the mapped distributions of $\mathbb{P}$ are represented as an element in the RKHS.

We extend their methods and apply them to a sentence retrieval task. Our method considers words comprising a query and a sentence as a set of words, and assumes that each word has a latent probability distribution mapped in a shared latent space. In other words, the query and sentence can be expressed as instances in an RKHS. Then, we calculate the similarity between the mapped sets in shared latent space using the kernel embeddings framework. In this paper, we use the word embeddings $\vec{w} \in \mathcal{X}$ trained by word2vec to represent a latent distribution.

The words embeddings $\vec{q_i}$ and $\vec{s_j}$ contained in query q and sentence s are the instances $\mu_{\mathbb{P}}$ on RKHS $\mathcal{H}_k$ determined by kernel k. Note that, in this paper, we treat word vectors as independent and identically distributed (i.i.d.). We show an instance of a query in the following RKHS. Instances of sentences are determined in the same manner.

$$\mu_{\mathbb{P}_q} = \frac{1}{|q|} \sum_{l=1}^{|q|} k(\cdot, \vec{q_l}) \in \mathcal{H}_k \qquad (1)$$

Here, we describe a method of measuring similarity between instances mapped on the RKHS. Assuming two sets of i.i.d. samples $X = \{x_l\}_{l=1}^{n}$ and $Y = \{y_{l'}\}_{l'=1}^{n'}$ existing in the same space, they are expressed as $\mu_{\mathbb{P}_X}$, $\mu_{\mathbb{P}_Y}$ by kernel embeddings representation. Moreover, the distance between the two distributions $D(X, Y)$ is calculated as follows:

$$D(X, Y) \;\; = ||\mu_{\mathbb{P}_X} - \mu_{\mathbb{P}_Y}||_{\mathcal{H}_k}^2 \qquad (2)$$

Therefore, the similarity sim_{ke} of the query and sentence is calculated by the inner-product $\langle \mu_{\mathbb{P}_q}, \mu_{\mathbb{P}_s} \rangle_{\mathcal{H}_k}$ in the RKHS as follows:

$$sim_{ke}(q, s) = \langle \mu_{\mathbb{P}_q}, \mu_{\mathbb{P}_s} \rangle_{\mathcal{H}_k}$$
$$= \frac{1}{|q||s|} \sum_{i=1}^{|q|} \sum_{j=1}^{|s|} k(\vec{q_i}, \vec{s_j}) \qquad (3)$$

Algorithm 1 Calculate Sentence Similarity

Input: sentence, query, N
Output: similarity
max_SIM $\leftarrow$ 0
for each N-gram (N= 1, 2, ..., N) $\in$ sentence
do
    SIM $\leftarrow$ sim_{ke}(query, N-gram)
    if SIM > max_SIM **then**
        max_SIM $\leftarrow$ SIM
    end if
end for
return max_SIM

2.2 N-gram Window

The kernel embeddings method is good at improving the recall of keyword-based sentence retrieval. However, owing to the canonical inner-product, it may decrease precision for a long sentence where keywords appear far apart. We propose a simple N-gram based method to overcome this challenge.

The algorithm is shown as Algorithm 1. First, our method delimits sentences by word N-grams. Second, we calculate the similarity between the query and each N-gram in the sentence. Finally, the highest similarity between the query and all N-grams is considered as the sentence similarity.

3 Experiment

3.1 Settings

As the latent vector, we used published word embeddings[1] learned by word2vec on part of a Google News dataset. To tokenize sentences, we used the Stanford Core NLP tokenizer (Ver. 3.6.0)[2]. Tokenized words were changed to lowercase to calculate similarity. We used the following cosine similarity and RBF kernel for k in Equation (3).

$$k_{cos}(q_i, s_j) = \frac{\langle q_i, s_j \rangle}{|q_i||s_j|} \qquad (4)$$

$$k_{\mathrm{RBF}}(q_i, s_j) = \exp\left(-\frac{||q_i - s_j||^2}{2\sigma^2} \right)$$
$$= \exp\left(-\gamma ||q_i - s_j||^2 \right) \qquad (5)$$

---

[1] https://code.google.com/archive/p/word2vec/
[2] http://nlp.stanford.edu/software/stanford-corenlp-full-2015-12-09.zip

Table 1: Example of pairs of query.

education innovative, identify research,
provide advice, plan annual,
recipient award, goal ensure,
partnership support, field industry,
improve success, lead experience

Preliminary experiments were performed using the hyperparameter γ of the RBF kernel within the range of $\gamma \in \{10^{-1}, 10^{0}, 10^{1}, 10^{2}\}$. We set the hyperparameter γ as $\gamma = 10^{1}$ based on the results.

3.2 Data

In this study, we experimented on a domain of academic press release articles. We constructed a sentence retrieval dataset for ESL in the following manner.

First, we created a corpus extracted from web pages containing ".edu" at the end of the domain name. We crawled the ".html" files up to three levels within the ".edu" domain, and used the text surrounded by p tags. The resulting corpus contained 579,867 sentences. We crafted 30 queries consisting of two words using a professional annotator, and extracted sentences from the corpus by exact matching of each query. The annotator evaluated whether the sentence was relevant to the query. The results were used as evaluation data.

Second, we picked ten queries with at least ten relevant sentences. As irrelevant sentences, we used 90 sentences that were deemed to be irrelevant by the annotator. When a query had less than 90 irrelevant sentences, we randomly sampled sentences from the evaluation data to increase this to 90 sentences. Note that all the relevant sentences used in this experiment contained two words. The average sentence length in the test data was 30 words. Table 1 lists the ten queries we used in testing.

3.3 Evaluation

We evaluated the result using Precision@k (hereafter, p@k), and compared our model with the following two baselines.

Average similarity. A simple baseline was calculated using the average similarity of the vectors of query and sentence. We used word2vec's word embeddings as the word vector. As the query vector, we averaged the word vectors of the query. Similarly, as the sentence vector, we averaged the word vectors of the words in the sentence. We compared these vectors using cosine similarity and RBF kernel.

Alignment-based similarity. As another baseline, we used one of the unsupervised sentence similarity measures proposed by Song and Roth (2015). These methods achieved state-of-the-art performance for a short text similarity (STS) task. We used their method to calculate the inter-sentence similarity (maximum alignment) based on the alignment in the distributed representation expressed by the following equation.

$$sim_{max}(q, s) = \frac{1}{|q|} \sum_{i=1}^{|q|} \max_{j} k(q_i, s_j) \quad (6)$$

This method calculates the maximum value of similarity between each keyword q_i of the query q and each word s_j included in the sentence s. Then, the similarity between the query and the sentence is calculated as the maximum value divided by the number of keywords $|q|$. We experimented with both cosine similarity and RBF kernel for k in Equation (6). Note that we did not symmetrize Equation (6).

3.4 Result

We show the results of the experiment in Figures 1 and 2. We calculated p@k from 1-gram to 40-grams and plotted the results of N-grams with an increment of ten, in addition to 1-gram to 5-gram. "Sentence" in figures refers to similarity based on all words in the sentence.

Figure 1 shows that when cosine similarity was used for the kernel, it was better not to use kernel embeddings. Further, alignment-based similarity is the most effective method, with the exception of the highest ranking. In this case, alignment-based similarity was better than almost all of the N-grams.

Figure 2 demonstrates that the accuracy of the RBF kernel increases with the incorporation of an N-gram window. In addition, the best result in the top-5 ranking was obtained by using RBF kernels and longer N-grams. These results indicate that the most effective RBF kernels have window sizes of 20-gram.

However, we observed that sizes of 1-gram to 3-gram produced a negative result for the RBF kernel. In the next section, we discuss why lower order N-grams led to negative results.

Table 2: Examples of a retrieved relevant sentence using a 19-gram, and an irrelevant one using cosine.

kernel	label	input query: partnership support
RBF	✓	The advisers work in *partnership* with the college staff and other university offices to provide information and *support* for all students and to offer programs on community issues as well as small-scale social activities.
Cosine	×	The Robert Mehrabian CIC is a *partnership* between Carnegie Mellon, the Carnegie Museums, and local economic development organizations and is funded with $8 million in Commonwealth of Pennsylvania tax *support*.

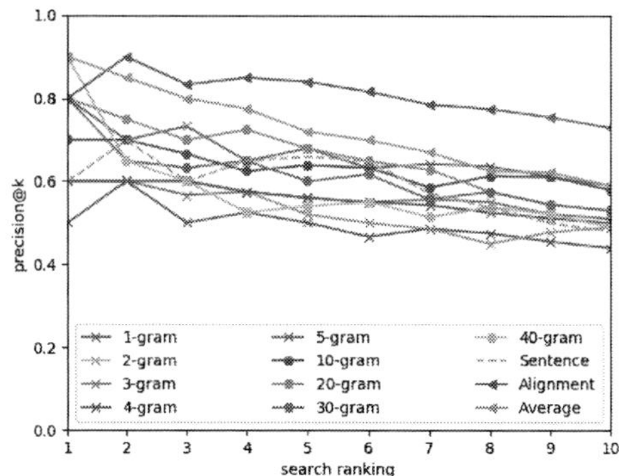

Figure 1: p@k of cosine similarity.

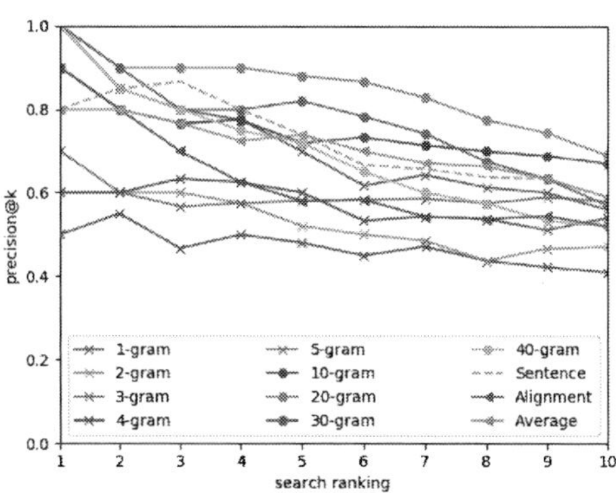

Figure 2: p@k of RBF kernel.

3.5 Discussion

We show the error analysis on the 19-gram RBF kernel, which exhibited the best score in the experimental results. Table 2 presents examples of one of the top-ten results of sentence retrieval. The topmost results of the proposed method comprise sentences relevant to the query. In contrast, the cosine baseline cannot consider latent intent; thus, it may output irrelevant sentences such as those without related keywords.

First, we measured the distance between words that match the query in the sentence of the test data exactly. The results show that the average distance between keywords was 11.8 words. In addition, for 72% of the gold sentences data, the keywords were found in the same clause. From these facts, we determined that useful sentences in this task were those in which keywords existed in the same clause, but were not located in close proximity. We regard this as one of the reasons why middle-sized N-grams were more effective.

Second, we compared alignment-based similarity with kernel embeddings. The former considers only the maximum similarity of words in the query and sentences. In contrast, kernel embeddings comprehensively considers all the words in the sentence. Furthermore, by combining this with the N-gram window approach, it is possible to focus on the surroundings of words with high similarity to the query. For these reasons, the kernel embeddings with N-gram window method outperforms alignment-based similarity.

4 Related Work

In recent years, many writing assistance systems have been developed. One of them is ESCORT, which is an English search system (Matsubara et al., 2008) for writing scholarly papers and survey reports; it aims to demonstrate examples of word usage. The input to this system is a sentence that will be parsed, and then the system will output sentences with the same syntactic structure. However, it assumes that there is a syntactic structure between keywords, which is not a valid assumption in our task. Further, latent intent of query is not modeled in their system.

In contrast, Chen et al. (2012) propose an English writing assistance system for ESL learners. The system, called FLOW, supplements the English vocabulary of non-English native speakers. If ESL learners cannot write in English owing to a lack of vocabulary, they can continue to write words in their first language within the sentence.

This system complements latent intent of query using their first language, whereas our approach improves sentence modeling using kernel embeddings.

In addition, Hayashibe et al. (2012) developed a tool to support English composition as the author writes. Like Chen et al. (2012), it accepts Romanized Japanese input in addition to English, to take the writer's first language into account. The tool can suggest a phrase considering context from the information already entered into the query. In contrast, we ask users to input only two words as a query. In addition, their example search system adopts an exact match approach, which may negatively impact the recall of the search system.

5 Conclusion

In this research, we proposed a new sentence retrieval method using a kernel embeddings framework to aid English composition. Our kernel embeddings method, using an RBF kernel and N-gram window, showed better results than two baseline methods (using cosine similarity and an alignment-based similarity). In future work, we aim to verify the effectiveness of our method for two or more queries.

References

Mei-Hua Chen, Shih-Ting Huang, Hung-Ting Hsieh, Ting-Hui Kao, and Jason S Chang. 2012. Flow: a first-language-oriented writing assistant system. In *Proceedings of the ACL 2012 System Demonstrations*, pages 157–162.

Yuta Hayashibe, Masato Hagiwara, and Satoshi Sekine. 2012. phloat : Integrated writing environment for ESL learners. In *Proceedings of the Second Workshop on Advances in Text Input Methods*, pages 57–72.

Shigeki Matsubara, Yoshihide Kato, and Seiji Egawa. 2008. Escort: example sentence retrieval system as support tool for English writing. *Journal of Information Processing and Management*, 51(4):251–259.

Alex Smola, Arthur Gretton, Le Song, and Bernhard Schölkopf. 2007. A Hilbert space embedding for distributions. In *Proceedings of International Conference on Algorithmic Learning Theory*, pages 13–31.

Yangqiu Song and Dan Roth. 2015. Unsupervised sparse vector densification for short text similarity. In *Proceedings of the 2015 Conference of the North American Chapter of the Association for Computational Linguistics: Human Language Technologies*, pages 1275–1280.

Yuya Yoshikawa, Tomoharu Iwata, Hiroshi Sawada, and Takeshi Yamada. 2015. Cross-domain matching for bag-of-words data via kernel embeddings of latent distributions. In *Advances in Neural Information Processing Systems 28*, pages 1405–1413.

Event Timeline Generation from History Textbooks

Harsimran Bedi[a*]   **Sangameshwar Patil**[b]   **Swapnil Hingmire**[b]   **Girish K. Palshikar**[b]
{bedi.harsimran, sangameshwar.patil}@tcs.com
{swapnil.hingmire, gk.palshikar}@tcs.com
[a]Department of CSE, IIT Patna, India
[b]TCS Research, Pune, India

Abstract

Event timeline serves as the basic structure of history, and it is used as a disposition of key phenomena in studying history as a subject in secondary school. In order to enable a student to understand a historical phenomenon as a series of connected events, we present a system for automatic event timeline generation from history textbooks. Additionally, we propose Message Sequence Chart (MSC) and time-map based visualization techniques to visualize an event timeline. We also identify key computational challenges in developing natural language processing based applications for history textbooks.

1 Introduction

With the advent of easy access to on-line educational content on the Internet through mobile and electronic reading devices, there is increasing trend of e-learning and hence creating resources that support e-learning. An important advantage of e-learning is it enables learners to do "any time, any place, any pace" learning (California Department of Education, 2012; Agrawal et al., 2013).

In this paper, we particularly focus on creating event timeline (or chronology) from history textbooks. Event timelines play an important role in understanding a historical phenomenon. It enables a student to situate her knowledge of history in relation to a spatio-temporal context.

De Keyser and Vandepitte (1998) identify different frames of reference that play a vital role in a student's understanding of a historical phenomenon:

1. *Chronological frame of reference*, which focuses on key phenomena and their significance over a period of time (e.g. key events in the *Renaissance*).

2. *Spatial frame of reference*, which focuses on key locations, geographies involved in the phenomenon (e.g., spread of the *Renaissance* across various parts of Europe)

3. *Social frame of reference*, which focuses on how the social fields such as politics, economics, culture, etc. interact within society during the phenomenon (e.g., social, cultural, religious characteristics of the *Renaissance*).

Stow and Haydn (2000) highlight importance of these frames of reference to develop a student's ability to ask and answer questions like "When did a particular phenomenon happen? What is its relevance to the present and the future? What are the key insights of it that should be learned?"

In this paper we primarily focus on the *Chronological* and *Spatial* frames of reference. We believe that it will also serve as a building block for the *Social* frame of reference. In this paper, we present a system for automatic event timeline generation from history textbooks. In addition to event timeline creation, we also propose two techniques for visualization of a timeline. The first technique uses Message Sequence Chart (MSC) (Rudolph et al., 1996) to highlight the interaction between multiple entities associated with a historical phenomenon. In the second technique, we first associate each event in a timeline with a time marker, a location, and one or more actors, and create a time-map to capture a spatio-temporal aspect of the timeline. An additional important goal of this paper is to identify key research problems in developing natural

---

[*] This work was done when the first author was at TCS Research, Pune.

Proceedings of the 4th Workshop on Natural Language Processing Techniques for Educational Applications, pages 69–77,
Taipei, Taiwan, December 1, 2017 ©2017 AFNLP

language processing based applications for history textbooks.

The paper is organized as: in Section 2 we give an overview of related work on timeline generation from a different type of text resources. In Section 3 we highlight important use-cases of event timelines. In Section 4 we propose our algorithm for timeline generation. Section 5 discusses two techniques for visualization of timelines. Experimental evaluation of generated timelines is an active area of research. In Section 6 we present preliminary results on validation of events having mention of time expressions. Section 7 discusses computational challenges in the construction of event timeline from NLP perspective. In Section 8 we conclude and discuss prospects of our work.

2   Related Work

Several authors (e.g. (Bamman and Smith, 2014; Palmero Aprosio and Tonelli, 2015; Ge et al., 2015)) have proposed use of encyclopaedic resources like Wikipedia in event time-line construction of historical figures and events. It is important to note that Wikipedia articles give a comprehensive overview of a historical phenomenon and try to cover all facts with hyperlinks and references to relevant material. Also, each Wikipedia article is focussed on one phenomenon, and it is likely to be authored independently of Wikipedia articles that it hyperlinks. So, it is highly possible that the authors of a Wikipedia article may assume that the reader has knowledge about other Wikipedia articles that it hyperlinks. This encyclopedic rigor may not be necessary for primary or secondary students, and such bombardment of facts may not encourage a student to obtain an interest in history. On the other hand, content in the textbooks is organized such that each section or chapter is focused on one concept and concepts are progressively introduced with specific learning goals (Agrawal et al., 2012).

Apart from Wikipedia, several authors have constructed timelines from social media like Twitter (e.g. (Alonso et al., 2017; Yao et al., 2016; Li and Cardie, 2014)) or news articles (e.g. (Zhou et al., 2016)). However, social media or news articles are not intended to be consumed by history students.

3   Use-Cases for Event Timeline for History Text

We identify following use-cases for event timelines from history text:

1. **Comparison of Timelines:**
   a) We can use timelines of two entities (e.g. kings or emperors) to understand similarity and differences between their lives. For example, a student or a historian would like to compare timelines of rulers who achieved power on their own at a young age, e.g., *Napoleon* and *Shivaji*[1]. The similarities in their lives as well as rise to power can be easily seen from their timelines e.g., both received military training early in their childhood. Both assumed leadership roles at a very young age. Napolean was officer at 16. Shivaji conquered the Torna fort and laid foundations of his kingdom at age of 15. They scored remarkable victories in their twenties. Napolean became Master of France at 30; whereas by age of 30, Shivaji, though not formally a king, had already established his rule over vast land of present day Maharashtra state of India. Both died in their early 50s.
   b) Timelines of two different dynasties or empires also can be used to compare their rise and fall (e.g., *First French empire* vs *Second French empire*).
   c) Comparison of timelines can be extended beyond entities such as kings or empires. For example, a student may be interested in comparison of two different civilizations e.g., the *Roman civilization* vs. the *Indus valley civilization.*

2. **Causal Analysis of Events:** Using textual clues and text entailment techniques from NLP combined with ordering of events from timeline can be used to infer causes or conditions that led to an event or a sequence of events: e.g., seeds of *World War II* were already sown at the end of *World War I*. Such a causal analysis can also be used for comparison of two event timelines. For example, *The Great Depression*[2] and *The Great Reces-*

---

[1] https://en.wikipedia.org/wiki/Shivaji
[2] https://en.wikipedia.org/wiki/Great_Depression

sion[3] are two major economic events that affected the world population. One would like to analyze the timelines of these two events and understand common or different causes of different events and their social, political, economic consequences.

3. **Pedagogical Applications:** We believe that event timelines and their formal representations can be used for creating pedagogical resources that will be useful for students as well as teachers of history. For example, students can use event timelines for question answering while teachers can use them for automatic question generation as well as automatic answer evaluation.

Developing solutions to the use-cases discussed above is part of future work. Our current focus is to (a) automatically generate event timelines using NLP tools and techniques, (b) develop solutions to visualize timelines that would help student to understand history using succinct representations.

4 Our Method

In this section, we give details of our proposed system.

4.1 Event Description

Defining an event for our system is crucial to our task. For the purpose of history textbooks, an event can be thought of an important thing that happened or took place at a certain point of time. It changed something or had some definite consequences in the physical world. For the purpose of this paper, we consider those events which are described by a verb. Verbs like *die, kill, defeat* are absolute physical action verbs giving a clear indication that something important happened. On the other hand, verbs like *consider, regard, think* are related with a psychological or mental action that did not happen in real. In this paper, we assume that an event represents an *activity, accomplishment, achievement, and change in physical state* (Vendler, 1957, 1967; Casati and Varzi, 2015).

4.2 Dataset Creation

To create a gold standard dataset, we annotated portions from following two history books – (i)

[3]https://en.wikipedia.org/wiki/Great_Recession

Chapter 5: Consolidation and Expansion of the Empire - Akbar (77 sentences) in *Medieval India: From the Sultanate to the Mughals* (Chandra, 2007) and (ii) *Chapter 23.3: Napoleon forges an empire* (113 sentences) from the book *World History* (Harker, 2012). The schema used for annotation is briefly described in Table 1. For every event, the schema consists of title, actors, locations, time/date expressions, and event description.

- `event title` (E_T) := title of the event, a succinct phrase capturing the gist of the event
- `actor i` $(A_i$ for $i = 0, 1, \ldots, n)$:= actors mentioned in the sentence
  - `actor type` (A_T) = {`person, organization`} := whether the actor is a person or an organization (e.g. *allies of World War II*[4] can be treated as an organization)
- `event time expression` (T) := the fragment of the sentence that represents temporal expression of the event
  - `time expression modifier` (T_M) = {`after, before, during, beginning, end, early, late`}
  - `time expression type` (T_T) = {`date, time, duration`}
- `location` (L) := the location at which the event happened
- `event verb phrase` (E_{VP}) := the verb phrase of the sentence that represents the event.

Table 1: Annotation Schema

Table 2 gives annotation of a few example sentences from (Chandra, 2007, Chapter 5).

4.3 Event Timeline Generation

The algorithm (Table 3) has three main steps. First, we extract the named entities in the text using Stanford CoreNLP (Manning et al., 2014). The PERSON and ORGANIZATION type named entities form the set of actors. The LOCATION entities give us spatial information about the events. Then we resolve the co-references of these entities. In the second step, we use SUTime temporal expression tagger (Chang and Manning, 2012) to extract the temporal expressions from the sentences having the mentions of actors or locations.

Our current system considers only those sentences for creating a timeline which contain at least one temporal expression. We name these sentence as "timeline sentences". We also provide facility to create an actor specific timeline genera-

ID	Sentence	Event title (E_T)
S_1	`[Early in 1576]`$_T$, `[Akbar]`$_{A_0}$ `[moved to]`$_{EVP}$ `[Ajmer]`$_L$.	*Akbar moved to Ajmer*
S_2	`[Akbar]`$_{A_0}$ `[deputed]`$_{EVP}$ `[Raja Man Singh]`$_{A_1}$ with a force of 5000 consisting of `[Mughals]`$_{A_2}$ and `[Rajputs]`$_{A_3}$ to lead a campaign against `[Rana Pratap]`$_{A_4}$.	*Akbar deputed Raja Man Singh against Rana Pratap*
S_3	In anticipation of such a move, `[the Rana]`$_{A_0}$ had `[devastated the entire region]`$_{EVP}$ upto `[Chittor]`$_L$ so that `[the Mughal forces]`$_{A_1}$ could get no food or fodder.	*Rana Pratap devastated the entire region upto Chittor*
S_4	`[The Rana]`$_{A_0}$ `[advanced with a force of 3000]`$_{EVP}$ from his capital at `[Kumbhalgarh]`$_L$.	*Rana Pratap advanced from his capital at Kumbhalgarh*
S_5	`[The Rana]`$_{A_0}$ `[took a position]`$_{EVP}$ near `[Haldighati]`$_L$, at the entrance of the defile leading to `[Kumbhalgarh]`$_L$.	*Rana Pratap took a position near Haldighati*

Table 2: Annotation of a few example sentences from (Chandra, 2007, Chapter 5)

tion. Given an actor, we filter those timeline sentences that mention the actor or have co-reference to the actor. In addition to named entities, we identify relations mentioned in a sentence using OpenIE component of Stanford CoreNLP (Angeli et al., 2015). We select the relation which has mentions of the maximum of a number of named entities as the title of the sentence. The algorithm for generating event timeline from a given piece of text is given in Table 3.

- **Input:** Chapter or Section of a history textbook : $\mathcal{C}$
- **Output:** Event timeline : $\mathcal{T}$: $\{e_1 \prec e_2 \prec e_3 \prec \ldots \prec e_N\}$, where $e_i = <$event title (E_T), actors (A), time expressions (T), location (L) $>$
- **Entity Extraction:**
  1. Identify named entities (e.g., person, organization, location) in each sentence in $\mathcal{C}$.
  2. Resolve the co-references of entity mentions.
  3. Extract set of sentences S which refer to these named entities from $\mathcal{C}$.
- **Time-Expression Extraction:**
  - Identify time expressions in each sentence in S.
- **Timeline Generation:**
  1. Let $S' \subseteq S$ such that each sentence in S' contains at least one time expression and at least an actor.
  2. Let $\mathcal{T}$ be initialized to empty timline.
  3. For each sentence $s \in S'$:
     (a) Let $A = \{A_0, A_1, \ldots, A_K\}$ be the list of actors mentioned in s
     (b) Let L = the location mentioned in s. (if no location mention in s, L = NULL)
     (c) Let T = the time expressions mentioned in the sentence
     (d) Identify relations between entities in s using OpenIE component of Stanford CoreNLP and select the relation with maximum number of named entities as title of the event (E_T)
     (e) Append tuple $e = < E_T, A, T, L >$ to $\mathcal{T}$
  4. Print event timeline $\mathcal{T}$.

Table 3: Algorithm for Timeline Generation

5 Visualization

Visualization of a timeline to promote better learning and understanding of students is highly relevant to this task. Features of a timeline like the flow of the events, the temporal and spatial elements of an event should be evidently clear in the visual output. We propose two techniques for visualization of a timeline.

5.1 Message Sequence Chart (MSC)

MSC is widely used for the visualization of message interchange of communicating entities with a communication system (Rudolph et al., 1996). An important goal of MSC is to do a visual abstraction of causal relations between events and participation of different entities within a communication system in these events. The diagram area of MSC involves two dimensions: vertical and horizontal. The vertical dimension represents time while the horizontal dimension represents entities.

It is important to note that a historical phenomenon is comprised of various entities (e.g., persons or organizations) and a set of ordered events. Hence, we believe that MSC can be used to visualize the timeline of a historical phenomenon such that the vertical or time dimension captures order of events that happened over a period, while the horizontal or entity dimension represents entities involved in these events. Currently, we manually create MSCs explicitly specifying the entities and the events. A sample MSC created using a MSC generator tool[5] for a sequence of events is shown in Figure 1. Following text from (Harker, 2012) was used while generating the MSC:

"In only four years, from 1795 to 1799, Napoleon rose from a relatively obscure position as an officer in the French army to become master of France. Napoleon Bonaparte was born in 1769

---

[5]`https://www.websequencediagrams.com/`

on the Mediterranean island of Corsica. When he was nine years old, his parents sent him to a military school. In 1785 , at the age of 16, he finished school and became a lieutenant in the artillery. When the Revolution broke out, Napoleon joined the army of the new government. In October 1795, fate handed the young officer a chance for glory."

In future, we would use APIs of the library to generate MSCs automatically.

5.2 Timeline with a Map (TimeMap)

As discussed earlier, the *spatial frame of reference* is important in a student's understanding of a historical phenomenon. Hence, towards the goal of enabling a student to realize the importance of geographical conditions of the location at which an event happened we propose a map based visualization system. For example, consider the following text from (Chandra, 2007, Chapter 5): *The battle of Haldighati (18 Feb. 1576) was mainly fought in the traditional manner between cavalrymen and elephants, since the Mughals found it difficult to transport any artillery, except light artillery over the rough terrain.*

It is important to note that *Haldighati* is a mountain pass in western India[6] and its geographical characteristics played a vital role in the *The battle of Haldighati*[7]. The example is illustrative in the sense that it emphasizes both temporal and spatial aspects in understanding the event: *The battle of Haldighati*.

We generate a time map for a given event timeline using *TimeMapper*[8]. The time map generated by TimeMapper can be embedded in an HTML page and can be easily viewed using a browser. For each event in a timeline we show its title, description and temporal expression and if the location of the event is available, then it is shown on the map. The events in a timeline can be browsed in sequential or random order by clicking on an event in the timeline. A sample event of a timeline can be seen in Figure 2.

6 Experimental Evaluation

Experimental evaluation of generated timelines is an active area of research. As mentioned earlier,

in this paper, we focus only on the sentences having mention of time expression. For the task of timeline generation, sentences with the time expressions are important as they enable relative ordering of events.

For the evaluation, we use the annotated portion from Chapter 5 (*Consolidation and Expansion of the Empire - Akbar*) from (Chandra, 2007). The dataset contains total 77 sentences having 1771 words. These sentences are linguistically complex. There are 22 words on average per sentence. Out of the 77 sentences, 27 sentences contain events with time expression. For the event detection task, the proposed algorithm achieves precision, recall and F1-measure of 0.647, 0.407 and 0.500 respectively.

We note here that this is a preliminary evaluation because we are considering only those events which are described by verbs. Further we have not tackled relative ordering of implicit time expression. For a more comprehensive generation and evaluation of event timelines, we need to address these and the other challenges identified in the Section 7. We recognize a more rigorous treatment for the same as a significant direction for future work.

7 Computational Challenges in Timeline Generation

The inherent nature of historical events along with its narration pose some specific challenges from NLP viewpoint. We incurred these challenges while annotating the data set and comparing it with the results obtained from our system. They are listed below:

7.1 Implicit temporal mentions and temporal co-reference

There are cases when a period is given but not in an explicit manner. In Table 4:R-1 we can observe that `the next twelve years` and `this period` refer to the time period of `1585-1592`. To place the corresponding event(s) on the timeline one needs to accurately resolve the explicit mention of `1585` to the above co-referring implicit time expressions.

7.2 Entity co-reference resolution

Co-reference resolution of entities (e.g., Person, Location, Organization) is a well-studied problem in NLP literature. In our proposed algorithm, we

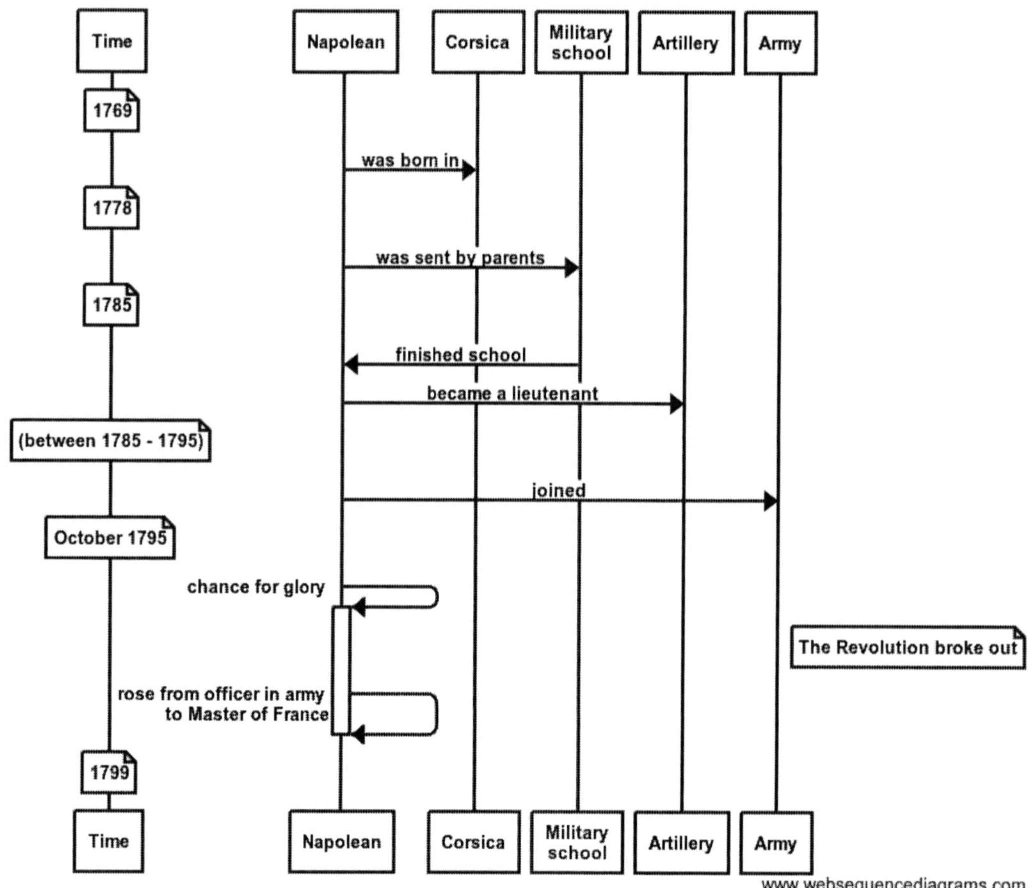

Figure 1: Multi-actor interaction visualization using Message Sequence Chart

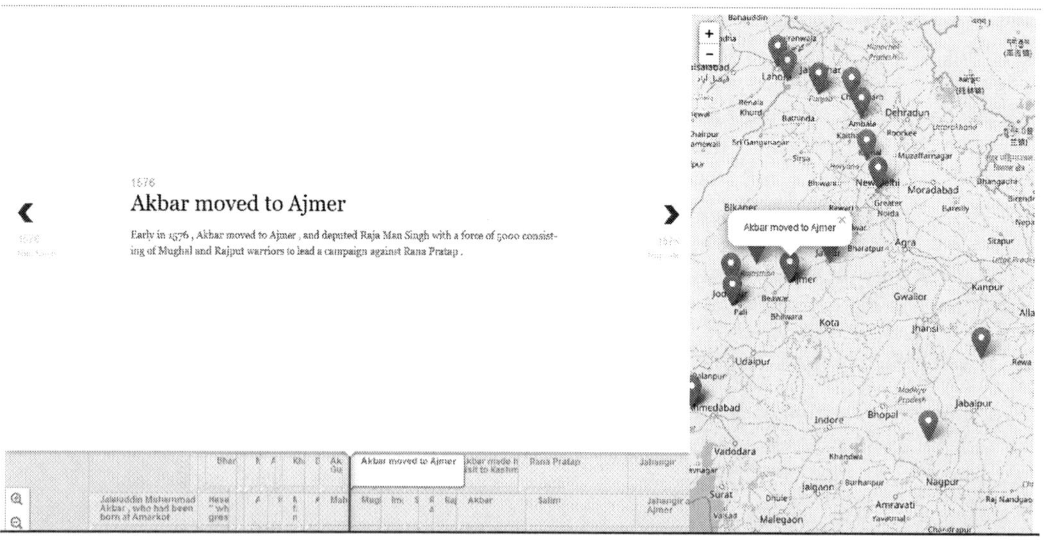

Figure 2: Sample screenshot of Time Map (spatio-temporal) corresponding to Table 1:S_1 sentence

R-1	**Implicit temporal mentions**	In 1585, Akbar moved to Lahore, and remained there for `[the next twelve years]`, watching the situation in the north-west. No Mughal expedition was sent against Rana Pratap during `[this period]`.
R-2	**Event coreference resolution**	Prince Salim was `[sent against]`$_{E1}$ the Rana in 1599, but achieved little. He was again deputed for `[the purpose]`$_{E1}$ in 1603, but he had no heart in `[the enterprise]`$_{E1}$. After his accession, Jahangir took up `[the matter]`$_{E1}$ more energetically.
R-3	**Inaccuracy due to wrong Entity coreference resolution**	`[Sagar]`$_{P1}$, `[the son of Rana Udai Singh]`$_{P1}$, `[who]`$_{P1}$ had joined `[Akbar]`$_{P2}$, during the rule of `[Rana Pratap]`$_{P3}$, and granted the title of Rana and installed at Chittor by `[Jahangir]`$_{P4}$, was set aside, and all the paraganas of Mewar, including Chittor were restored to `[Rana Amar Singh]`$_{P5}$.
R-4	**Normalization of named entities**	`[He]`$_{P1}$ died in 1597 at the young age of 51, due to an internal injury incurred by him while trying to draw a stiff bow. ... `[Prince Salim]`$_{P2}$ was sent against `[the Rana]`$_{P1}$ in 1599, but achieved little. `[He]`$_{P2}$ was again deputed for the purpose in 1603, but `[he]`$_{P2}$ had no heart in the enterprise. After `[his]`$_{P2}$ accession, `[Jahangir]`$_{P2}$ took up the matter more energetically.
R-5	**Hierarchy of events**	Sagar, the son of Rana Udai Singh, who `had joined Akbar`, during the rule of Rana Pratap, and `granted the title` of Rana and `installed at Chittor` by Jahangir, `was set aside`, and all the paraganas of Mewar, including Chittor `were restored` to the Rana.
R-6	**Location as an actor**	At the time of Napoleon's coup, France was still at war. In 1799, `[Britain, Austria, and Russia]` joined forces with one goal in mind, to drive Napoleon from power.

Table 4: Examples of computational challenges from NLP perspective faced while processing of history text

use entity-centric co-reference annotator component of Stanford CoreNLP (Clark and Manning, 2015).

In Table 4:R-3, we see the gold-standard coreferences for a sample sentence. The state-of-the-art Stanford CoreNLP coreference algorithm is not able to identify any of the gold-standard coreferences and incorrectly identifies a coreference between the phrases `Rana Pratap` and `Rana` (in the phrase "title of Rana"). For timeline generation task these errors in co-reference resolution have a cascading effect on the accuracy of actor, location identification etc. This results in incorrect events participants on the timeline.

7.3 Event co-reference resolution

Apart from the person/entity level co-reference resolution, history text poses very interesting co-reference resolution challenges at event level. In Table 4:R-2, `sent against` is an event involving two entities `Prince Salim` and `the Rana`. This event (*E1*) is referred to as `the purpose`, `the enterprise`, `the matter` in the subsequent lines.

7.4 Normalization of entity names

In the historical domain, a person of importance has many names or titles throughout his/her life-time.

- **Title resolution:** With reference to the Rajputs[9], *The Rana* was a standard epithet given to the current heir of the Rajput dynasty. In (Chandra, 2007, Chapter 5), initially the title `the Rana` is used to refer to `Rana Pratap Singh`. Further in the chapter his son `Rana Amar Singh` is referred to by the same title. In Table 4:R-4, `He` and `the Rana` refer to `Rana Pratap` according to the output of Stanford CoreNLP Co-Reference Annotator. But in real, `the Rana` refers to `Rana Amar Singh`.

- **Multiple names to same person:** Another case of this challenge arises when two names are used for the same person like *Jahangir*[10] is also referred to as *Prince Salim*.

- **Location standardization:** The problem of standardization is also applicable to locations. Cities or states names mentioned in history might have been replaced with new names at present. This poses a problem when it comes to locating that place on a map. For

[9] https://en.wikipedia.org/wiki/Rajput
[10] https://en.wikipedia.org/wiki/Jahangir

example the state of *Mewat*[11] mentioned in (Chandra, 2007, Chapter 5) does not exist on India's map.

7.5 Hierarchy of events

The task of event extraction is a complicated one. In simple sentences the event verb and its arguments are clear. But if we look at Table 4:R-5, hierarchy within events is observed. In this example `was set aside` is the key event, however, phrases like `Sagar joined Akbar`, `granted the title`, `installed at Chittor`, `were restored`, etc. indicate related and sub-events of the key event.

7.6 Location-Actor ambiguity

There are many instances where a location is associated with event verbs which are applicable on actors. For example in Table 4:R-6, the countries `France, Britain, Austria, Russia` are not locations, rather they are actors of type organization.

7.7 Event title generation

While visualizing a timeline instead of showing a complete event sentence, it is more useful to generate and show a short and succinct title for each event. However, generating such a title is challenging.

Events in text are typically described using verbs. One straight-forward approach to generate title of an event could be to use the main action verb and its associated subject(s) and object(s). However, in many cases, events are also described using non-verbal (e.g, nominal) expressions. For instance, consider the sentence `_ The Great Depression` lasted from `1929 to 1939`. Here the event `The Great Depression` occurs in nominal form.

In other cases, event sentences may contain multiple sub-events (e.g., Table 4:R-5). They can be associated with actors, location, time/date, relations or with other events. So it is important to identify the different kinds of events to come up with a succinct title describing the complete event.

7.8 Evaluation

There are three important aspects on which an automatically generated timeline should be evaluated. The first aspect is precision and recall of events extracted from the text. This aspect mainly does an evaluation of event extraction component of timeline generation algorithm. The second aspect is an evaluation of title generation and extraction of relevant named entities from text. The third aspect is an evaluation of order of events in an automatically generated timeline. It is important to note that these three aspects are interlinked to each other. Hence, it necessitates appropriate evaluation measure(s) for timeline evaluation that will collectively consider the three aspects discussed above.

There is also need of live user studies where students of history participate to evaluate utility of timeline visualization techniques in understanding historical phenomena. We will explore both empirical and user evaluation of timeline generation in the future.

8 Conclusions and Future Work

In this paper, we propose a system for generation of event timeline from history textbooks. We also propose two techniques to visualize a timeline. Message Sequence Chart based visualization enables a student to observe involvement of multiple actors in a historical phenomenon. On the other hand, time-map based visualization enables a student to understand spatio-temporal aspects. We believe that both these visualization techniques will increase a student's interest and curiosity in learning history as a subject. Hence, in addition to a working system, we also identify key computational challenges in creating NLP based applications for history subject. Of course, the system proposed in this paper can be improved across many dimensions. Currently, we are generating a timeline specific to a human actor. In the future, we would like to generate a timeline for a non-human actor, e.g., a timeline of *art or science in the Renaissance*. We also aim to define annotation guidelines for annotation of historical events and release a much larger annotated dataset that can be used for various tasks such as entity/event extraction and segmentation, co-reference resolution of named entities as well as events.

References

Rakesh Agrawal, Sunandan Chakraborty, Sreenivas Gollapudi, Anitha Kannan, and Krishnaram Kenthapadi. 2012. Quality of textbooks: an empirical study. In *ACM Annual Symposium on Computing*

---

for Development, ACM DEV '12, Atlanta, GA, USA - March 10 - 11, 2012, page 16:1.

Rakesh Agrawal, Sreenivas Gollapudi, Anitha Kannan, and Krishnaram Kenthapadi. 2013. Studying from electronic textbooks. In *22nd ACM International Conference on Information and Knowledge Management, CIKM'13, San Francisco, CA, USA, October 27 - November 1, 2013*, pages 1715–1720.

Omar Alonso, Serge-Eric Tremblay, and Fernando Diaz. 2017. Automatic generation of event timelines from social data. In *Proceedings of the 2017 ACM on Web Science Conference, WebSci 2017, Troy, NY, USA, June 25 - 28, 2017*, pages 207–211.

Gabor Angeli, Melvin Jose Johnson Premkumar, and Christopher D. Manning. 2015. Leveraging linguistic structure for open domain information extraction. In *Proceedings of the 53rd Annual Meeting of the Association for Computational Linguistics and the 7th International Joint Conference on Natural Language Processing of the Asian Federation of Natural Language Processing, ACL 2015, July 26-31, 2015, Beijing, China, Volume 1: Long Papers*, pages 344–354.

David Bamman and Noah Smith. 2014. Unsupervised discovery of biographical structure from text. *Transactions of the Association for Computational Linguistics*, 2:363–376.

California Department of Education. 2012. Education technology task force work group facilitators.

Roberto Casati and Achille Varzi. 2015. Events. In Edward N. Zalta, editor, *The Stanford Encyclopedia of Philosophy*, winter 2015 edition. Metaphysics Research Lab, Stanford University.

Satish Chandra. 2007. *Medieval India: From Sultanat to the Mughals- Mughal Empire: Part Two*. Har Anand Publications.

Angel X. Chang and Christopher D. Manning. 2012. Sutime: A library for recognizing and normalizing time expressions. In *Proceedings of the Eighth International Conference on Language Resources and Evaluation, LREC 2012, Istanbul, Turkey, May 23-25, 2012*, pages 3735–3740.

Kevin Clark and Christopher D. Manning. 2015. Entity-centric coreference resolution with model stacking. In *Proceedings of the 53rd Annual Meeting of the Association for Computational Linguistics and the 7th International Joint Conference on Natural Language Processing of the Asian Federation of Natural Language Processing, ACL 2015, July 26-31, 2015, Beijing, China, Volume 1: Long Papers*, pages 1405–1415.

R. De Keyser and P. Vandepitte. 1998. *Historical formation. Design of vision*. Flemish Board for Catholic Secondary Education, Brussel, Belgium.

Tao Ge, Wenzhe Pei, Heng Ji, Sujian Li, Baobao Chang, and Zhifang Sui. 2015. Bring you to the past: Automatic generation of topically relevant event chronicles. In *Proceedings of the 53rd Annual Meeting of the Association for Computational Linguistics and the 7th International Joint Conference on Natural Language Processing of the Asian Federation of Natural Language Processing, ACL 2015, July 26-31, 2015, Beijing, China, Volume 1: Long Papers*, pages 575–585.

Shieh Harker. 2012. World History II. https://worldhistoryii. wordpress.com/2012/10/12/ 23-3-napoleon-forges-an-empire/. Accessed: 2017-08-23.

Jiwei Li and Claire Cardie. 2014. Timeline generation: tracking individuals on twitter. In *23rd International World Wide Web Conference, WWW '14, Seoul, Republic of Korea, April 7-11, 2014*, pages 643–652.

Christopher D. Manning, Mihai Surdeanu, John Bauer, Jenny Rose Finkel, Steven Bethard, and David McClosky. 2014. The stanford corenlp natural language processing toolkit. In *Proceedings of the 52nd Annual Meeting of the Association for Computational Linguistics, ACL 2014, June 22-27, 2014, Baltimore, MD, USA, System Demonstrations*, pages 55–60.

Alessio Palmero Aprosio and Sara Tonelli. 2015. Recognizing biographical sections in wikipedia. In *Proceedings of the 2015 Conference on Empirical Methods in Natural Language Processing*, pages 811–816, Lisbon, Portugal. Association for Computational Linguistics.

Ekkart Rudolph, Peter Graubmann, and Jens Grabowski. 1996. Tutorial on message sequence charts. *Computer Networks and ISDN Systems*, 28(12):1629–1641.

William Stow and Terry Haydn. 2000. Issues in the teaching of chronology. In *Issues in history teaching*. London ; New York : Routledge.

Zeno Vendler. 1957. Verbs and times. *The Philosophical Review*, 66(2):143–160.

Zeno Vendler. 1967. *Linguistics in Philosophy*. Cornell University Press.

Jin-ge Yao, Feifan Fan, Wayne Xin Zhao, Xiaojun Wan, Edward Y. Chang, and Jianguo Xiao. 2016. Tweet timeline generation with determinantal point processes. In *Proceedings of the Thirtieth AAAI Conference on Artificial Intelligence, February 12-17, 2016, Phoenix, Arizona, USA.*, pages 3080–3086.

Deyu Zhou, Haiyang Xu, Xin-Yu Dai, and Yulan He. 2016. Unsupervised storyline extraction from news articles. In *Proceedings of the Twenty-Fifth International Joint Conference on Artificial Intelligence, IJCAI 2016, New York, NY, USA, 9-15 July 2016*, pages 3014–3021.

Author Index